BestMasters

Springer awards „BestMasters“ to the best master's theses which have been completed at renowned universities in Germany, Austria, and Switzerland.
The studies received highest marks and were recommended for publication by supervisors. They address current issues from various fields of research in natural sciences, psychology, technology, and economics.
The series addresses practitioners as well as scientists and, in particular, offers guidance for early stage researchers.

Franziska Eller

The Effectiveness of Neurofeedback Training for Children with Autism Spectrum Disorders

Springer

Franziska Eller
Potsdam, Germany

BestMasters
ISBN 978-3-658-08289-5 ISBN 978-3-658-08290-1 (eBook)
DOI 10.1007/978-3-658-08290-1

Library of Congress Control Number: 2014957959

Springer

Printed on acid-free paper

Springer is a brand of Springer Fachmedien Wiesbaden
Springer Fachmedien Wiesbaden is part of Springer Science+Business Media
(www.springer.com)

Foreword

The number of children that have been diagnosed with an Autism Spectrum Disorder (ASD) has increased considerably in recent years. Primarily, genetic factors are discussed as being the causes of this neurodevelopmental disorder. Neuropsychological research indicates an abnormal development of the brain, causing deficient brain functions. The few existing scientifically proven treatment approaches for ASD are mainly behavior-based. In spite of conspicuous deviations in the brain wave activity and the increasing implementation of biofeedback therapy, Neurofeedback training is not yet significantly considered as a therapy approach for treating ASD.

In this evolving research context Franziska Eller conducted a quasi-experimental study in order to investigate the effectiveness of Neurofeedback training in addition to a basic neurodevelopmental treatment for children with ASD. The multi-methodical approach used included EEG and test data of the participants as well as behavior assessments by their parents and teachers. This extensive research design has not been applied under laboratory conditions, but has been implemented in an actual treatment setting. Thereby the author added an important contribution to the limited number of existing studies in this field of research.

The results of the study indicate that, in contrast to the control group, children who received an additional Neurofeedback training showed clinically significant improvement in prior abnormal brain wave activity. The Neurofeedback sessions were aimed at identifying and training each child's individual abnormalities in the brain wave activity patterns. A decrease of autistic behavioral peculiarities was observed in the participants of both groups, while children receiving an additional Neurofeedback training showed a greater reduction of mannerisms. These conclusions can serve as a reasonable basis for future studies. However, a direct relation between the changes in the brain wave activity and the behavior of the children could not be established.

With her methodical approach and an innovative strategy of data analysis, Franziska Eller deserves credit for presenting a reasonable guideline for future research projects in the practical context of treatment for children with ASD. The findings are promising enough to justify an intensification of corresponding research efforts and also to consider Neurofeedback training as a feasible treatment option for Autism Spectrum Disorders.

Prof. Dr. Daniela Hosser
Technische Universität Braunschweig

Acknowledgments

First of all, I would like to thank the Jacob's Ladder Neurodevelopmental School and Therapy Center in Roswell, Georgia for giving me the opportunity to conduct a research study at their facility. Thank you for your trust and confidence in allowing me to work independently and to take responsibility for conducting and completing the study. Your constant support was greatly appreciated. It was my pleasure to work with such an open-minded and dedicated team. A special thank you to Mrs. Karla Brigiotta, Neurofeedback practitioner at the Jacob's Ladder Center. Thank you for all the extra time spent, the many additional hours of Neurofeedback training with the children, the numerous parent meetings and all other efforts made in order to conduct the project successfully. I truly appreciated the endless support for and commitment to my ambitious ideas.

Thank you to my academic supervisor, Prof. Dr. Daniela Hosser for the unconditional support of my research ideas and for the assistance from near and far.

Finally, I would like to thank my parents and the many others who helped make my ideas become reality. Your tremendous support, patience and encouragement during the last year were highly appreciated.

Thank you.

Franziska Eller
October 2014

Abstract

The study investigated the effectiveness of Neurofeedback training for Autism Spectrum Disorders (ASD) in addition to a basic neurodevelopmental therapy. The research design aimed at examining if children, aged 4.0-14.3 years, receiving Neurofeedback training showed improvements over time and if they could achieve greater improvements than a control group due to the additional training. Sixteen participants with an ASD diagnosis were assigned to a treatment ($n = 8$) or control group ($n = 8$). Both groups received an intense basic therapy, while the treatment group additionally participated in 15 sessions of Neurofeedback training based on individualized training protocols. Progress was assessed using quantitative electroencephalography (QEEG) recordings, two autism questionnaires as well as an imitation test. Furthermore, assessments by parents and teachers were compared in order to explore if changes were seen similarly by different respondents. Results revealed that all participants showed improvements in several domains. Especially a successful reduction in autistic mannerisms was reported, measured by the Social Responsiveness Scale (SRS-2). However, participants of the treatment group could partly achieve greater improvements than the control group, particularly regarding their imitation abilities as well as their brain wave activity. The QEEG data of the treatment group explicitly revealed positive changes after the Neurofeedback training. Both, parents and teachers comparably reported improvements, which could indicate possible generalization effects to different environments. The results clearly speak for the benefits of combining a comprehensive basic therapy with a supplemental Neurofeedback training for treating ASD effectively. Limitations of the study and implementations for future research investigations are discussed.

Table of contents

Tables and figures

1 Introduction

Autism Spectrum Disorders (ASD) contain a wide range of social, behavioral and communicative impairments that can appear within a certain range of severity. The number of children diagnosed with an Autism Spectrum Disorder is rising yearly. *Autism Speaks*, a non-profit organization in the United States, published official facts on its website stating that "autism now affects 1 in 88 children" and that "autism is the fastest-growing serious developmental disability in the U.S." (2013). This noticeable increase can result from different reasons that are discussed controversially by experts (Rutter, 2005; Pasco, 2010). Generally, an actual increase of the incidence of ASD is possible. Furthermore the improvement of diagnostic tools and methods can also help to identify more cases of Autism Spectrum Disorders (Rutter, 2005). On the other hand, the increasing public interest and awareness of the disorder may also lead to the problem of over diagnosing behavioral abnormalities as an ASD (Frances, 2011). Further research on these issues is needed to clarify the real causes of the increasing number of diagnoses.

In any case, the rising number of affected individuals causes a high demand for beneficial ways of treatment. This is challenging due to the vast diversity of autistic symptoms. Current research studies aim to identify effective interventions for all concerned persons. To this day, only three treatment programs can be considered as evidence-based approaches (level of evidence IIa; Bölte, 2009): the *Applied Behavior Analysis* (Lovaas, 1981, 1987), the *Treatment and Education of Autistic and related Communication handicapped Children (*TEACCH; Schopler, Mesibov, & Hearsey, 1995) and the *Picture Exchange Communication System* (PECS; Bondy & Frost, 1994). Extended future endeavors are also needed in the fields of causal research since possible sources still could not be identified completely. However, by now it is generally accepted that Autism Spectrum Disorders are often caused by genetic abnormalities or deviances in the brain structure and function (Autism Society, 2013; APA, 2013; Nickl-Jockschat & Michel, 2011). The goal of Neurofeedback is to improve the ability of the patients to self-regulate the activity of their brain waves (Congedo, Lubar, & Joffe, 2004). Its potential to directly approach neurobiological dysfunctions (Niv, 2013) is an important advantage of this method. It became increasingly important in the last decades as a form of intervention that can be successfully used for the treatment of many disorders and disabilities, such as attention deficit hyperactivity disorder, autism, brain injuries and posttraumatic stress disorder (e.g. Peniston & Kulkolsky, 1991; Gevensleben et al., 2009; Larsen, 2012). Considering this it seems reasonable to examine and research Neurofeedback training as an effective therapy approach to not only reduce autistic symptoms, but in fact to change and redirect the causative abnormal brain activity.

The present study transferred current research investigations to a new context. The effectiveness of a Neurofeedback training as an additional intervention to a neuro-developmental therapy approach was examined. All participating children received a daily basic treatment at the Jacob's Ladder Center, a specialized therapy center for children with neurological disorders. The treatment group received 15 additional sessions of Neurofeedback training. In order to investigate the effectiveness of this supplemental therapy element, quantitative electroencephalography data (QEEG), the performance on an imitation test as well as questionnaires filled out by parents and teachers were analyzed. This variety of assessment instruments was convenient to evaluate the children's progress on a neurodevelopmental, behavioral and functional level.

2 Theoretical background and current research situation

Autism Spectrum Disorders are characterized by impairments regarding communication, interaction and behavior (APA, 2013). In the following the valid diagnostic criteria for ASD are introduced as well as a short overview concerning important therapy approaches and selected research findings, with the goal of integrating Neurofeedback into the current treatment and research situation. Subsequently, the procedure of Neurofeedback training is explained and important advantages of this treatment approach are discussed. Finally, results of empirical studies on the effectiveness of Neurofeedback training for Autism Spectrum Disorders are presented.

2.1 Autism Spectrum Disorder

According to the Diagnostic and Statistical Manual of Mental Disorders (DSM-5; APA, 2013), the Autism Spectrum Disorder (299.00) belongs to the group of Neuro-developmental Disorders. The manifestation of an ASD begins early in the individual development and is characterized by deficits that typically remain persistent across the life-span. Unlike other disorders of that group, which only impact specific skills or functioning, the diagnosis of an ASD describes the existence of more extensive impairments regarding several functional aspects (ibid.). Individuals show restricted communication and interaction skills as well as linguistic impairments that can range up to a complete absence of language development. Additionally, distinctive behavioral features are characterized by repetitive motor mannerisms, restricted interests or the compulsive insistence on unchanging daily routines and environmental attributes (Sinzig, 2011).

The recently published DSM-5 contains an important revision of the previously valid diagnostic criteria of the DSM-IV-TR (APA, 2000). One of the most significant changes is that there is no longer any differentiation among four separate disorders. The former DSM-IV-TR diagnoses of Autistic Disorder (299.00), Asperger's Disorder (299.80), Pervasive Developmental Disorder Not Otherwise Specified (PDD-NOS, 299.80) and Childhood Disintegrative Disorder (299.10) are now integrated in the DSM-5 diagnosis of an Autism Spectrum Disorder. The main characteristics of the ASD are now described with two core symptom groups, with the requirement that attributes of both areas have to be present. Since the DSM-5 features some significant changes regarding the diagnosis of an Autism Spectrum Disorder, table 1 presents an overview of the current valid diagnostic criteria. This chart is also an explanation basis for the outcome measures used for the study. Independently of each other, both main symptom groups can vary in their severity, also referred to as the individual manifestations on the spectrum. To specify the extent of the particular impairments, both main diagnostic criteria need to be rated on a severity scale with three levels. These levels indicate if support (1), substantial support (2) or very substantial support (3) is required (APA, 2013). In addition, the diagnosis of an Autism Spectrum Disorder also includes further specifications, such as an accompanying language or intellectual impairment, the existence of other associating mental disorders or given genetic and medical conditions (ibid.).

Table 1: New diagnostic criteria for the Autism Spectrum Disorder (Excerpt from the Diagnostic and Statistical Manual of Mental Disorders (DSM-5); APA, 2013)

AUTISM SPECTRUM DISORDER 299.00 (F.84.0)

Diagnostic Criteria

A Persistent **deficits in social communication and social interaction** across multiple contexts, as manifested by the following, currently or by history:

1. Deficits in social-emotional reciprocity, ranging, for example, from abnormal social approach and failure of normal back-and-forth conversation; to reduced sharing of interests, emotions, or affect; to failure to initiate or respond to social interactions.
2. Deficits in nonverbal communicative behaviors used for social interaction, ranging, for example, from poorly integrated verbal and nonverbal communication; to abnormalities in eye contact and body language or deficits in understanding and use of gestures; to a total lack of facial expressions and nonverbal communication.
3. Deficits in developing, maintaining, and understanding relationships, ranging, for example, from difficulties adjusting behavior to suit various social contexts; to difficulties in sharing imaginative play or in making friends; to absence of interest in peers.

B Restricted, repetitive patterns of behavior, interests, or activities, as manifested by at least two of the following, currently or by history:

1. Stereotyped or repetitive motor movements, use of objects, or speech (e.g., simple motorstereotypies, lining up toys or flipping objects, echolalia, idiosyncratic phrases).
2. Insistence on sameness, inflexible adherence to routines, or ritualized patterns of verbal or nonverbal behavior (e.g. extreme distress at small changes, difficulties with transitions, rigid thinking patterns, greeting rituals, need to take same route or eat same food every day).
3. Highly restricted, fixated interests that are abnormal in intensity or focus (e.g., strong attachment to or preoccupation with unusual objects, excessively circumscribed or perseverative interests).
4. Hyper- or hyporeactivity to sensory input or unusual interest in sensory aspects of the environment (e.g., apparent indifference to pain/temperature, adverse response to specific sounds or textures, excessive smelling or touching of objects, visual fascination with lights or movement).

C Symptoms must be present in the early developmental period (but may not become fully manifest until social demands exceed limited capacities, or may be masked by learned strategies in later life).

D Symptoms cause clinically significant impairment in social, occupational, or other important areas of current functioning.

E These disturbances are not better explained by intellectual disability (intellectual developmental disorder) or global developmental delay. Intellectual disability and autism spectrum disorder frequently co-occur; to make comorbid diagnoses of autism spectrum disorder and intellectual disability, social communication should be below that expected for general developmental level.

An important reason for considering and investigating Neurofeedback training as an effective treatment for ASD is the non-satisfying fact that numerous existing therapy approaches are not yet evidence-based. They also often cannot meet the needs of this heterogeneous patient group (Perry & Condillac, 2003). Currently there are only a few treatment approaches for ASD whose effectiveness has been empirically supported (level of evidence IIa), including the *Applied Behavior Analysis* (ABA), the *Treatment and Education of Autistic and related Communication handicapped Children (*TEACCH) and the *Picture Exchange Communication System* (PECS) (Bölte, 2009). The ABA (Lovaas, 1981, 1987) uses principles of classic and operant conditioning to modify behavior, basically by teaching and reinforcing desired behavior, as well as simultaneously reducing and fading out problem behavior. The TEACCH approach (Schopler et al., 1995) also aims at teaching behavioral and cognitive skills to enhance independency and decrease negative behavior. An important attribute of this treatment is the creation of an individually adapted and structured environment for the patients to facilitate the therapeutic work. The PECS method (Bondy & Frost, 1994) is especially helpful for nonverbal or minimally verbal children as it teaches the use of picture cards in order to express themselves and to communicate with others. This system can easily be combined with other treatments as an additional therapy component. As mentioned earlier, there are many more therapy methods, some more promising than others (Poustka, Bölte, Feineis-Matthews, & Schmötzer, 2004), whose effectiveness needs to be investigated in future research endeavors. Neurofeedback training certainly is an approach with a great potential. Initial support of successful implementations has already been established and will be cited later.

The finding of effective treatments is directly linked to the research regarding the actual causes of Autism Spectrum Disorders. Research studies have still not completely identified all possible sources. However, several scientific studies found that ASDs primarily have genetic causes (Meyer-Lindenberg, 2011). These genetic mutations can be high risk factors for an abnormal development of the brain, for example, by inhibiting the formation of important neuronal connections (ibid.) or by causing inadequate brain wave activity (Pop-Jordanova, Zorcec, Demerdzieva, & Gucev, 2010). These deviant patterns can lead to severe deficits in neuropsychological functions and abilities, such as executive functions, central coherence, theory of mind, language, intelligence and imitation abilities (Sinzig, 2011). Children usually begin to imitate gestures, facial expressions or actions including objects at a very young age. This is an important precondition for the development of the Theory of Mind, which is the ability to be aware of and comprehend internal thoughts and emotions, and those of others (ibid.). In children diagnosed with an ASD these abilities often are limitedly evolved (Rogers, Hepburn, Stackhouse, & Wehner, 2003). Therefore autistic individuals often show difficulties in planning and controlling their own behavior or in recognizing complex social situations. It can be very challenging to identify and understand emotions, thoughts or intentions (Sinzig, 2011). Numerous research studies investigated the neuropsychological functioning of people with autism (for a review see for example Dziobek & Köhne, 2011), and by now many experts agree that a dysfunctional mirror neuron system is one of the main causes for limited neurocognitive abilities (e.g. Poustka et al., 2004; Oberman et al., 2005; Pineda et al., 2008). This system controls perception and recognition of basic motor actions, but is presumably also involved in more complex cognitive processes and thereby may lead to the impairments described above (Rizzolatti, Fogassi, & Gallese, 2001; Oberman et al., 2005). Furthermore, scientists have detected that certain brain areas of people with an ASD are over- or under-aroused during cognitive processing, compared to normally functioning brains (Dziobek & Köhne, 2011). At times completely different areas become activated for cognitive performances, such as working memory or executive functions. This indicates the development of compensatory strategies in the autistic brain (ibid.). Another phenomenon often mentioned in the literature describes that cerebral functions are not sufficiently integrated and therefore different psychological functions cannot be coordinated correctly (Lautenbacher & Gauggel, 2010). This results in the often observable deficits in processing, integrating or reacting appropriately to perceptions, emotions or behaviors. Therefore it appears to be reasonable to research Neurofeedback as a form of intervention that is aimed at fundamentally changing the functioning of the brain.

2.2 Neurofeedback training

Neurofeedback, also called EEG biofeedback, is a computerized treatment approach for neurobiological dysfunctions that aims at modifying abnormal brain activity. By receiving immediate information about the neuronal patterns, individuals can learn to regulate the activity of their own brain waves based on operant conditioning (Thatcher, 2009). In the course of time, researchers developed several Neurofeedback training programs that partly differ in their recordings and possible training methods. A comprehensive description of these various programs would unfortunately exceed the framework of this paper. However, all approaches are based on the general principles of providing instantaneous feedback on recorded brain activity, with the objective of redirecting deviating brain waves to a designated range. This change is in turn "associated with positive changes in physical, emotional, and cognitive states" (International Society for Neurofeedback and Research, 2010). In the following a detailed explanation of the *Z-Score Neurofeedback Training* (Thatcher, 2009) is provided, as this is the form of training that was used in the present study.

The fundamental idea of this approach is the permanent comparison of the recorded brain activity to a normative database, therefore also referred to as QEEG (quantitative electro-encephalography). The QEEG signals deviations from normative metrics and thus can be used to identify the targets for the training (Larsen, 2012). Through 19 electrodes that are connected to the scalp (figure 1), the EEG activity of the brain is recorded. Figure 2 shows the positioning of all electrodes according to the International 10/20 System of electrode placement

(Jasper, 1958). Each electrode registers wave frequencies, this raw data is then divided into frequency bands via fast Fourier transformation. The power spectrum contains of the following known frequencies: delta (1-4 Hz), theta (4-8 Hz), alpha (8-12 Hz) beta (12-25 Hz) and high beta (25-30 Hz). Table 2 presents a short description of the different frequency bands and associated correlates, as well as consequences of abnormal occurrence.

Figure 1: Cap with 19 electrodes measuring brain wave activity
(Source: Jacob's Ladder Center)

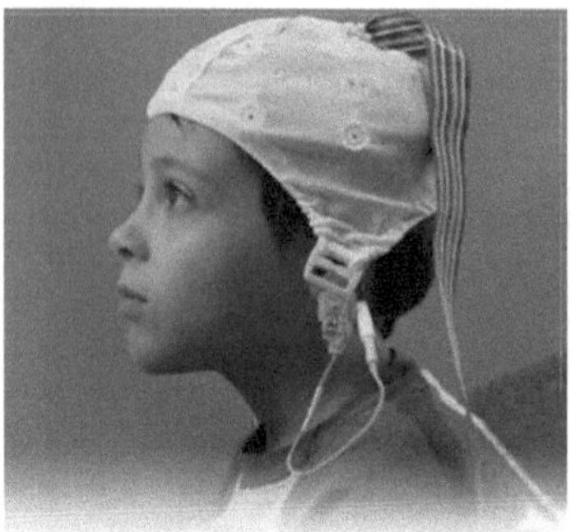

Figure 2: Labeling of the 19 electrode positions on the scalp
(Note: A1 and A2 only serve as reference electrodes)
(Source: http://ionm.pro/2011/11/12/ american-clinical-neurophysiology-society-practice-guidelines-eeg-ep-iom/)

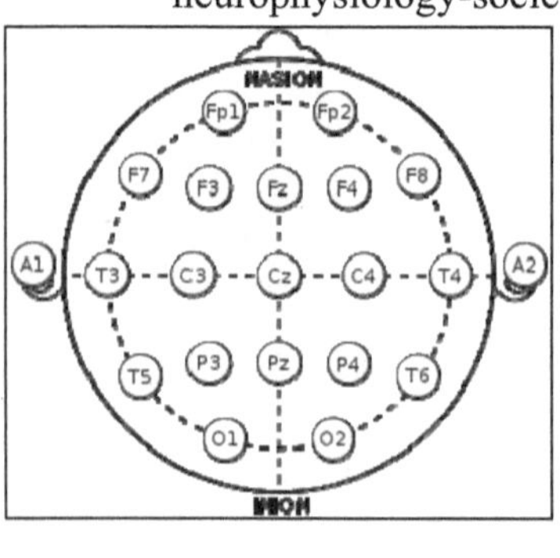

Table 2: Overview of the brain frequency bands and their occurrence (adapted from Robbins, 2008; Neurohealth Associates, 2004)

Frequency Band	**Related Brain States**	**Associated Behavior**	**Physiological Correlates**	**Possible effects of abnormal occurrence**
Delta (1-4 Hz)	deep, dreamless sleep, trance, unconscious	lethargic, not attentive	low level of arousal	too much delta and/or theta can limit the ability to focus, concentrate and maintain attention; can interfere with learning and memory
Theta (4-8 Hz)	hypnogogic state, consciousness between sleep and deep relaxation	daydreaming, creativity, internal focus	integration of mind and body	
Alpha (8-12 Hz)	relaxed, but awake	no action, mental resourcefulness, resting	relaxed, calm, alert, but not actively processing information	more/less alpha can cause abnormal sensations, deficiencies in self-control
Beta (12-25 Hz)	normal waking consciousness	mental activity: listening, thinking, decision making	alert, active, but not agitated	too much beta and/or high beta can increase alertness, tension, mental stress or anxiety; less beta/high beta can cause a lack of focused attention, emotional instability
High Beta (25-30 Hz)	alertness, high concentration	mental activity: math, planning, analytical problem solving	general activation of mind and body functions	

The fragmented data is quantitatively compared to a matching normative group, featuring the same age, gender and handedness as the patient, in order to identify abnormalities (Larsen, 2012). The values are then converted into z-scores, facilitating the estimation of deviations. Previously to the beginning of the actual

Neurofeedback training, the data is merged to a brain map, summarizing the data visually and numerically. Figure 3 shows an example of a brain map (topographic presentation). The electrodes record information about the following dimensions: absolute power of the frequency bands (voltage, measured in microvolt), the relative power (represented amount of each frequency band), as well as the amplitude asymmetry (balance of the brain activity between the different areas), the coherence (connection and communication between the different areas) as well as the phase lag (timing of the energy transfer) (Thatcher, 2009). Taking into account all this information, considerable abnormalities can be identified easily and, consequentially, the goals for the Neurofeedback training can be defined.

For the actual training, the threshold for the target frequency and dimension needs to be set. Several target frequencies, dimensions and electrode positions can be selected at the same time, but this increases the difficulty of the training as several activity patterns need to be adapted simultaneously in order to be rewarded. At the beginning of the training the threshold value is usually set at a relatively low level, in order to have the subject experience successful participation. This process can be seen as a form of operant conditioning, since the reinforcement is only obtained when the desired brain wave activity is shown (Larsen, 2012). In the course of the training, the threshold value is raised to higher levels, aiming at a movement towards a low z-score that indicates no or only minimal deviations from the norm. With the help of a special computer program the permanently recorded raw data can be converted to auditory and visual signals, simultaneously representing the brain signals (Congedo et al., 2004). This apparent feedback can help to increase the patient's awareness of his or her own brain activity and to learn how to modify it. To enhance the success and Neurofeedback experience for younger patients – as the ones in the present research project – the feedback can be displayed in an age-appropriate way, for example in the form of a movie or video game that only plays when the brain wave activity appears as desired.

Figure 3: Topographic brain maps representing the QEEG data
The dots symbolize the 19 electrodes on the scalp; the colors illustrate the severity of the deviation (indicated in z-scores, see legends for details). A clear image would represent normal functioning concerning the particular frequency and target dimension.

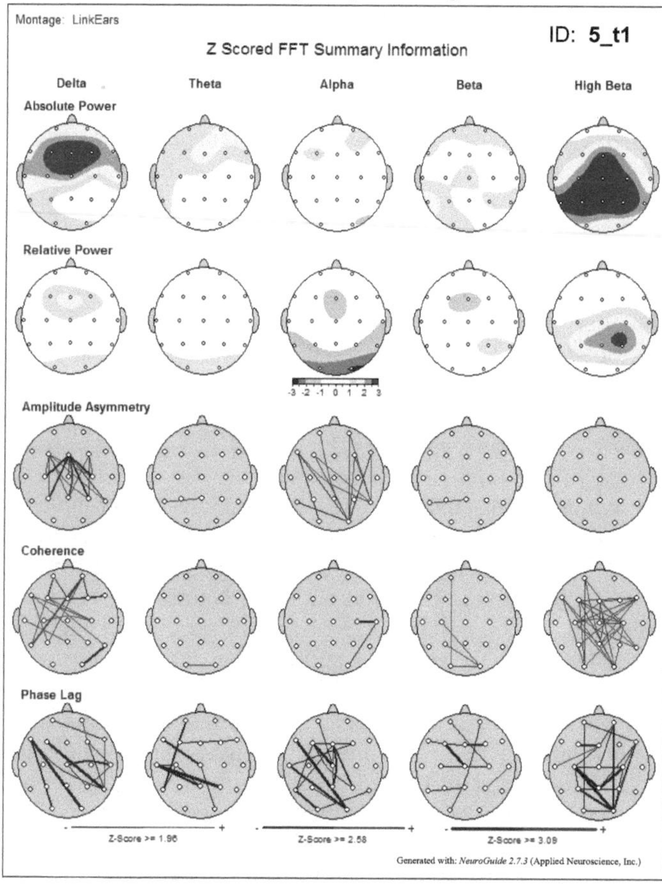

In this example the absolute power (voltage) of delta and theta is distinctively increased, especially in the frontal and left temporal area. The absolute power of high beta is expansively highly increased. Alpha frequencies are significantly underrepresented in the occipital area, while high beta frequencies are overrepresented in the central, parietal and temporal areas. (During the recording of the EEG data the subject was awake, but relaxed, no instruction for a mental activity was given.)

Besides the previously described standard surface Neurofeedback, researchers developed another, more advanced approach in the last years that can analyze deeper into the brain. With the help of LORETA (Low Resolution Electromagnetic Tomography) a 3-dimensional localization of problem areas in cortical and subcortical regions is possible. Specific brain areas and functional systems can be identified more precisely and thereby an even better targeted training is possible (Robbins, 2008; Larsen, 2012).

Neurofeedback training is a cost-intensive method that still needs further systematic empirical evidence of its effectiveness. However, there are several advantages that should be considered as they depict Neurofeedback as a promising approach for numerous disorders, such as Attention Deficit Hyperactivity Disorder, Autism Spectrum Disorder, anxiety, brain injuries or Post-Traumatic Stress Disorder (e.g. Peniston & Kulkolsky, 1991; Gevensleben et al., 2009; Larsen, 2012). In contrast to many other therapies, Neurofeedback training aims at changing the individual's brain activity fundamentally, instead of only treating the symptoms of a disorder. It is a noninvasive approach, thus the brain cannot become dependent on outside influences like medication or electric impulses (Niv, 2013). For these reasons it is likely that Neurofeedback can create long-term effects, which can remain persistent even after the termination of the training. First studies found evidence for long-term effects of positive changes in the brain wave activity (e.g. Abarbanel, 1995; Kouijzer, de Moor, Gerrits, & Buitelaar, 2009b). Moreover, Neurofeed-back training sessions are completely individualized, based on the subject's recorded brain activity and the accompanying symptoms, which is an important requirement especially concerning treatment approaches for ASD (Bölte, 2009). In addition, Neurofeedback training is adjustable at any time, for example in case of the worsening of symptoms or similar occurrences. Moreover, to date no side effects from Neurofeedback training have been reported (Coben, Linden, & Myers, 2010). Another important benefit is the possibility of combining Neurofeedback training with other treatment approaches to potentially increase the therapy progress. Thatcher (2009) describes several specific advantages of the real-time z-score training, including a simplification of the data analyses as different metrics (power, coherence etc.) are converted into common z-scores. He also states that this form of training provides a definite threshold ($z = 0$) and a clear direction of change, as the goal of this treatment is a movement of the EEG towards a healthy reference group (ibid.).

2.3 Neurofeedback training for Autism Spectrum Disorders

As stated earlier, Neurofeedback training is currently implemented to treat many different conditions. The best evidence of its effectiveness is given for Attention Deficit Hyperactivity Disorder as it has been investigated in numerous research studies in the last years. Arns, de Ridder, Strehl, Breteler and Coenen (2009) published a meta-analysis on the efficacy of Neurofeedback training for ADHD and found medium effect sizes concerning hyperactivity and large effect sizes for inattention and impulsivity. They stated that the clinical effects of Neurofeedback training can be considered clinically meaningful in the field of ADHD treatment. To date, the research findings regarding the effectiveness of Neurofeedback training for ASD are not as extensive and partly ambiguous (Billeci et al., 2013). Inconsistent study results lead to debates on the application of Neurofeedback. In a recently published review Holtmann et al. (2011) stated that the use of Neurofeedback training for ASD is not supported by existing studies and that future investigations need to clarify which symptoms can actually be reduced with this form of treatment. However, several published studies presented promising results and are an important impulse for broader research intentions in the future.

The first pilot study was conducted by Jarusiewicz (2002) and included a total of 24 children. The experimental group (*n* = 12) underwent a mean of 36 Neurofeedback sessions (range = 20-69). The Neurofeedback training was based on established protocols for other disorders with similar symptoms. To evaluate the efficacy of the training, parental ratings of autism symptoms on the Autism Treatment Evaluation Checklist (ATEC) as well as assessments of problem behavior were used. An average 26% reduction in the total ATEC autism symptoms was reported for the children who received the Neurofeedback training, compared to 3% reduction for the control group. Parents also reported reductions of problem behavior, such as anxiety, tantrums or schoolwork, while only minimal changes were reported for the control group.

So far, the largest controlled study was published by Coben and Padolsky (2007), examining assessment-guided Neurofeedback for ASD. 49 children were matched for different attributes and either assigned to a treatment group (*n* = 37) or a wait-list control group (*n* = 12). Each subject in the treatment group received Neurofeedback training twice a week for a total of 20 sessions. Treatment protocols were individualized and based on the initial QEEG assessments, with a special focus on connectivity abnormalities. A variety of assessment instruments were used to measure the effects of the training, including parental judgment of outcome, neurobehavioral rating scales, several tests of neuropsychological functioning and QEEG analyses. In the treatment group 89% of the parents observed a decrease of ASD symptoms, which signified a high success rate, while in the control group 83% reported no change. Parent ratings measured by questionnaires showed a 40% reduction of ASD symptoms in the treatment group over time. Additionally, children who received Neurofeedback training improved significantly on several neuropsychological measures, such as tests for visual perceptual functioning and attention.

Pineda et al. (2008) conducted two studies, examining if Neurofeedback training can normalize mu suppression and improve behavior in children with ASD. Suppression of mu rhythms (7-10 Hz), which are an EEG measure of resting motor neurons, occurs during observation of actions or execution of movements. Abnormal mu rhythms characterize dysfunctional mirror neuron activity (Cochin et al., 1998). In study 1 (Pineda et al., 2008), eight male participants (age 7-17) with high-functioning autism were assigned to an experimental (n = 5) or placebo group (n = 3) at random. One participant in the experimental group dropped out during the course of the study. Changes due to 30 sessions of Neurofeedback training were measured with different autism questionnaires, cognitive assessments and QEEG analyses. Results showed that the children in the treatment group learned to successfully control their mu rhythms. Concerning the imitation abilities, both groups improved over time, but no significant difference between the groups was found. Parent ratings on the Autism Treatment Evaluation Checklist (ATEC) revealed a significant increase of the experimental group in sensory/cognitive awareness, compared to a decrease of the placebo group. The procedure of study 2 was similar to the first one. The sample was larger, with 9 children in the experimental and 10 children in the placebo group, who were randomly assigned. Participants' diagnoses of high-functioning autism were verified with two autism questionnaires and an intelligence test prior to the beginning of the study. Neurofeedback training and assessments of changes were similar to study 1. Results indicated a stronger effect on behavior and QEEG parameters in the experimental group. But, in contrast to many improvements in the experimental group that were seen by the parents, they also perceived a distinctive negative change in sensory/cognitive awareness that did not occur in the placebo group. Again, both groups partly improved in their imitation behavior, but no interaction effect was found.

Kouijzer, de Moor, Gerrits, Congedo and van Schie (2009a) conducted a study to investigate the benefit of Neurofeedback training for executive functioning. 14 children (8-12 years) were assigned to a treatment or a control group, matched by gender, age and intelligence. The treatment group received 40 Neurofeedback sessions. The goal of the training was to reduce theta activity (4-7 Hz) and to simultaneously increase SMR activity at the scalp location C4 (SMR = *sensorimotor rhythm*, activity in the low beta band, 12-15 Hz). Changes were assessed by analyses of the QEEG data, a range of executive function tasks as well as an autism and a communication questionnaire. Five of the seven children receiving the Neurofeedback training were able to successfully adjust their brain wave activity according to the protocol. However, compared to the control group, no significant changes in the QEEG data of the treatment group were found. Only the children in the treatment group showed large improvements in the tasks for attentional control, goal setting and cognitive flexibility. Parent ratings revealed an increase in communication skills and social interaction. A 12-month follow-up study (Kouijzer et al., 2009b) indicated possible long-term effects of Neurofeedback interventions, as the improvements of social behavior and executive functioning were maintained. Based on these findings, Kouijzer et al. (2010) conducted a further study, implementing some methodological improvements. They allowed inclusion of children with more severe forms of ASD and individualized the Neurofeedback protocols based on the QEEG findings. Participants were randomly assigned to the treatment (n = 10) and control group (n = 10). Furthermore, the 40 Neurofeedback training sessions were implemented in the children's school programs in order to reduce the investment for the participating families. Besides parent ratings of social behavior, teacher ratings were collected as well, aiming at investigating behavioral improvements in different contexts. Again, parents reported an increase in social interactions and communication skills after the Neurofeedback training, compared to minor changes in the control group. A 6-months follow-up (ibid.) revealed that the improvements in the treatment group were still sustained. These significant enhancements observed by parents were not found in the teacher ratings. Regarding the QEEG data, 60% of the participants successfully reduced excessive theta activity in the designated frontal and central target areas and sustained beyond the termination of the training sessions.

The selected studies reveal outcomes that are mainly positive and support the assumption that Neurofeedback training is an effective intervention for children diagnosed with an Autism Spectrum Disorder. However, further research is necessary to draw final conclusions as the presented studies have many limitations (Billeci et al., 2013). These will be discussed later, in connection with limitations regarding the present study.

The present study intended to combine several of the reasonable methods and instruments utilized in the described studies. In order to be able to research new aspects concerning the effectiveness of Neurofeedback training, investigations were transferred to a new context. All participants attended the same therapy center and thus all treatment and control group members received a basic therapy. For this reason, the present study investigated if Neurofeedback as a supplemental treatment can enhance the progress that is achieved with the basic treatment. Furthermore, parents and teachers were asked to rate their children or students (cf. Kouijzer et al., 2010). Since all teachers worked at the same therapy center, these assessments were better comparable among each other. Also the ratings could be compared more easily to the parent ratings in order to detect possible effects of generalization to different environments.

3 Research questions and hypotheses

The goal of the research project was to investigate the possible benefit of Neurofeedback training in addition to a basic neurodevelopmental treatment at the Jacob's Ladder Center. Due to the fact that all children received a basic neurodevelopmental treatment, it was expected that all participants' assessments improved over time. In addition, it was assumed that the participants who received an additional Neurofeedback training showed greater improvements in neurological, behavioral and functional aspects. This resulted in the following research questions and hypotheses:

Research Questions:

1. Do children who receive an additional Neurofeedback training show greater improvements in neurological, behavioral and functional aspects than children who only receive a basic neurodevelopmental treatment?
2. Do the assessments of the children by their parents differ from the assessment by their teachers of the Therapy Center?

Hypotheses:

H1: All participants will show a reduction in their autistic symptoms over the time of the research project, identifiable with all assessment instruments.

In comparison to the control group, after 15 NFB sessions (respectively after an equal time duration) participants who receive an additional NFB training…

H2: …will show significantly less deviation in their brain wave activity from normative data, identifiable with their QEEG data.

H3: …will be rated significantly lower in their autistic symptoms and other attendant deficiencies, measured by the *Social Responsiveness Scale (SRS-2)* and the *Autism Treatment Evaluation Checklist ATEC.*

H4: …will show significantly greater improvements in their ability to follow verbal directions, to imitate gestures and to use tools correctly, measured by the *Florida Apraxia Screening Test, Revised (FAST-R).*

In addition to these hypotheses, the following supplemental research questions concerning the participants who receive NFB sessions will be exploratively investigated:

H5: Do the participants' parents rate them significantly lower in their autistic symptoms after the implementation of the 15 NFB sessions, measured by the *SRS-2* and *ATEC*?

H6: Do the participants' teachers rate them significantly lower in their autistic symptoms after the implementation of the 15 NFB sessions, measured by the *SRS-2* and *ATEC*?

H7: Do the assessments of the children by their parents significantly differ from the assessment by their teachers, measured by the *SRS-2* and the *ATEC*?

4 Method

The present study was conducted at the Jacob's Ladder Neurodevelopmental School and Therapy Center in the United States. The study design and conception were independently planned and implemented by the author of this thesis. This included the selection and adaption of the assessment instruments, the contacting of all considered families, the coordination and distribution of the questionnaire material as well as the conduction of the imitation test.

4.1 Participants

To select the participants for the study, all actively enrolled children with a current diagnosis of an Autism Spectrum Disorder were identified. The diagnoses were given by child psychologists or psychiatrists previous to the admission of the patients at the therapy center. All eligible participants were diagnosed prior to the publication of the DSM-5. Therefore all children who had diagnoses of Autism Disorder, Asperger's Disorder and PDD-NOS according to the formerly valid DSM-IV-TR were included, based on the fact that all these children would most likely also meet the DSM-5 criteria for an Autism Spectrum Disorder (APA, 2013b). A total of n = 16 eligible children (12 males, 4 females) with a mean age of 8.2 years (range 4.0-14.3 years) could be identified. Information sheets describing the project (appendix A) were sent to the parents who then could choose if they wanted their child to participate either with or without receiving an additional Neurofeedback intervention. Based on these consents the treatment group (n = 8) and control group (n = 8) were created. Due to the relatively small sample, no further criteria for exclusion were set. The only stated requirement was that none of the participants could have ever had any Neurofeedback interventions in the past. This was necessary to ensure that all children received the same number of treatment sessions, as well as to exclude possible existing long term effects. Three of the participating children were nonverbal, but were able to hear and understand speech, which was important since many of the instructions during the assessments were given orally. One participant was on stable medication before and during the whole inquiry period. She was included in the examination as there were was no change in the dosage and therefore no enhancement of the treatment effect caused by medication was assumed. Seven children received additional weekly treatment sessions outside of the therapy center, such as speech therapy or occupational therapy. None of these were neurological approaches and thus they were not expected to interfere with the Neurofeedback training. Therefore all of these children were included in the examination. Appendix F displays an overview of all participating subjects, their diagnoses and other relevant characteristics.

4.2 Procedure

For this study a non-randomized pre-test-post-test design with one treatment group and one control group was used. The study protocol was approved by the ethics committee (Faculty 2) at the University of Technology Braunschweig, Germany. At the beginning of our study, baseline data from every participant was collected in multiple ways. A brain map of every child was recorded to receive QEEG data describing their brain wave activity. Regrettably two participants were very sensitive to any unexpected sensation on their scalp and strongly resisted the use of the caps, hence it was impossible to record their brain maps. Parents and the main therapist of each child were asked to fill out two questionnaires describing characteristics of the child's behavior, language, skills and physical as well as emotional conditions (appendix B). Additionally a test to evaluate imitation abilities was conducted with every participating child.

During the conduction of the study all participating children received a treatment based on the intervention approach which is implemented at the therapy center. This comprehensive basic treatment uses a "brain-based methodology incorporating targeted neurodevelop-mental interventions" (Jacob's Ladder Center, 2013, p.1). These interventions consist of exercises and techniques to improve the individual neurodevelopmental functioning of each child, including gross motor, fine motor, language, tactility, auditory and visual skills. The extensive treatment is supposed to lead to a progress in neurocognitive abilities, such as sequential and working memory, concept formation, focus and attention, decision speed, planning ability or retrieval fluency (Jacob's Ladder Center, 2013b). Furthermore, the therapy center also considers physiological aspects, individual learning style characteristics as well as emotional, social and behavioral distinctions in order to develop customized treatment programs to meet the individuals' needs, abilities and challenges in the best possible way (ibid.).

The students in the treatment group additionally received two sessions of Neurofeedback training every week over a period of eight weeks, and finished after a total of fifteen sessions per child. The number of sessions is a required minimum in order to be able to determine changes in the assessment instruments. Before the beginning of the intervention, all parents of the treatment group members were invited to a personal meeting. This was done in order to educate them about the procedure of Neurofeedback training. During the meeting the brain maps of their children were presented and individually preferred goals were discussed. All sessions occurred during the presence of the children at the therapy center, so there was no additional effort for the participating families. The intervention was based on the Z-Score Neurofeedback Training as described earlier. All sessions were conducted and monitored by a qualified Neurofeedback practitioner. An individual training protocol (Coben & Padolsky, 2007) for every participant was created, based on the results of the initial QEEG data recording as well as the specific goals discussed with the parents. Minor adjustments during the process were allowed if needed. The procedure itself was also individualized by adapting the duration of the sessions and the reinforcement level to the needs and the abilities of the children. This strategy aimed at achieving the greatest benefits and progress possible for each participant (Thatcher, 2009). The focus was on training the absolute and relative power of the different frequency bands (see figure 3), hence only these two dimensions were included in the analysis of the QEEG data. For reinforcement preferred movie scenes as well as animated video files provided by the *NeuroGuide* program (Applied Neuroscience, Inc.) were used. The set-up of the Neurofeedback training is displayed in figure 4.

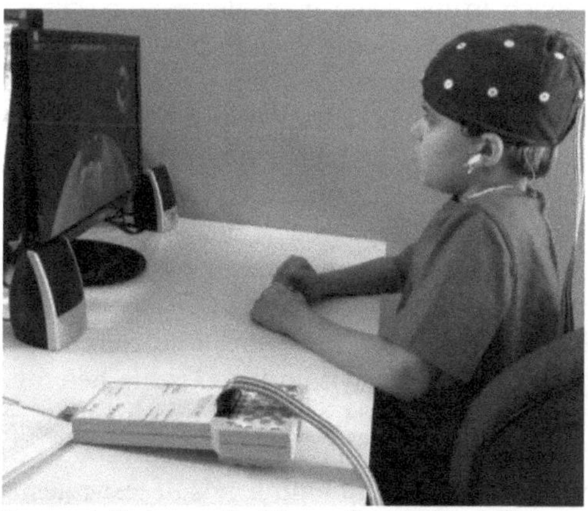

Figure 4: Set-up of a Neurofeedback training session. The movie scene on the screen only plays when the desired brain wave activity is shown. The performance is monitored by a practitioner on a second screen. (Source: Jacob's Ladder Center)

After conclusion of the intended fifteen Neurofeedback sessions for the treatment group and a comparable time interval for the control group, the parents and main therapists of the participants were asked to complete the same two questionnaires they had also received at the beginning of the study (appendix C). The test on imitation abilities was repeated. To receive updated QEEG data on the individual brain wave activity, a second brain map of all 16 participants was recorded.

4.3 Assessment instruments

To obtain a comprehensive evaluation of autistic symptoms and attending abnormalities, assessments on a neurological, behavioral and functional level were conducted. With the help of questionnaires, tests and QEEG data it was possible to collect subjective and objective ratings.

4.3.1 QEEG

To assess the brain wave activity, quantitative EEG data was recorded and summarized into brain maps, as described earlier in detail. For the creation of the brain map, as well as for the actual training, the software *NeuroGuide 2.7.3* (Applied Neuroscience, Inc.) was utilized. A stretchable electrode cap with 19 electrode sensors (cp. figure 1) was attached to the scalp with electrode paste, and two ear clips were used as reference electrodes. Sensors were positioned based on the International 10/20 System of electrode placement using the *TruScan 32 Acquisition EEG System* (Deymed Diagnostic). The duration of the EEG recording varied between 10 and 15 minutes. The data was then examined manually by the practitioner and afterwards scanned and adjusted automatically by the *NeuroGuide* software, in order to receive an artifact-free data set. The raw data was then transformed to z-scores as described earlier. The normative database of *NeuroGuide* consists of 625 subjects with an age range from 2 months to 82 years (Thatcher, Biver, & North, 2007). These z-scores were used for the data analysis, since the raw scores were not comparable within the existing heterogeneous sample. As stated earlier, the focus of the training was on adjusting the absolute and relative power, therefore only these z-scores were analyzed to detect improvements. Numerous scientific studies found high levels of test-retest as well as split-half reliability for QEEG. The content validity was ascertained by high correlations with independent measures, such as MRI, SPECT or neuropsychological tests (ibid.). The reported values for reliability and clinical validity were higher than .95 and have been established for many different psychological and psychiatric disorders (Thatcher, 2010).

4.3.2 Social Responsiveness Scale (SRS-2)

The SRS-2 (Constantino & Gruber, 2012) is a four-point Likert-scale, containing 65 items that measure autism related symptoms. All statements need to be rated whether they are "not true", "sometimes true", "often true" or "almost always true". The items cover five areas of behavior: social awareness (e.g. "Expressions on his or her face don't match what he or she is saying."), social cognition (e.g. "Doesn't understand how events relate to one another (cause and effect) the way other children his or her age do."), social communication (e.g.: "Is able to communicate his or her feelings to others."), social motivation (e.g. "Would rather be alone than with others.") as well as restricted interests and repetitive behavior (e.g. "Has repetitive, odd behaviors such as hand flapping or rocking."). The total score, including all items, describes if the inquired behavioral patterns are within normal limits or indicate a mild, moderate or severe form of an Autism Spectrum Disorder. The higher the scores, the more severe are the impairments. The SRS-2 also provides two subscales that are compatible with the updated DSM-5 criteria, describing the two main symptom domains of Autism Spectrum Disorders: *Restricted Interests and Repetitive Behavior* (RRB, 12 items) as well as *Social Communication and Interaction* (SCI; calculated as the sum from the remaining 4 parts; 53 items total). For the statistical analyses of the present study, the questionnaires filled out by parents and teachers were separately included. Furthermore, 'general' scores were created by calculating item values as the mean of both parent and teacher rating of the corresponding items. The scale was originally normed using the primary five subsets on a total clinical sample of 7,921 individuals (aged 4-18), of which $n = 4{,}891$ were clinical subjects (Constantino & Gruber, 2012). Overall alpha internal consistency was very high at .95. No internal consistency values for the subsets were reported. The authors refer to several studies that reported test-retest reliabilities ranging from $r = .88$ to .95 (ibid.). Therefore a high level of stability, which is required for pre-/post-treatment assessments, can be assumed. Regarding the convergent validity, high correlations with other important behavior assessments (e.g. Social Communication Questionnaire) and with diagnostic instruments for ASD (e.g. Autism Diagnostic Observation Schedule) were reported, many of those ranging around correlations of .60 or higher (ibid.). Initial validation evidence supporting the two DSM-5 compatible subscales was also reported: confirmatory factor analyses (e.g. Frazier et al., 2012) support a two-factor approach (ibid.). For this reason, the calculation of this study's results is based on the scores of two subscales and the total score.

4.3.3 Autism Treatment Evaluation Checklist (ATEC; modified)

The ATEC (Rimland & Edelson, 1999) was designed to evaluate the effectiveness of treatments for Autism Spectrum Disorders. The original version was used as a basis for this study, but some item sections were altered and a few items were added in order to create a more comprehensive questionnaire that matches all DSM-5 criteria for ASD. Furthermore, the modification of the checklist aimed at recording all important characteristics of the participants that could possibly be influenced by the Neurofeedback training, but were not included in the original version of the ATEC (item example: "Bothered by textures on body, face or hands, having nails cut, hair combed."). The final, Likert-scaled questionnaire consisted of 4 scales: *(I) Language and Communication* (18 items, e.g. "Explains what he/she wants."), *(II) Sociability and Interaction* (24 items, e.g. "Seems to be in a shell – you cannot reach him/her."), *(III) Behavior and Interest* (24 items, e.g. "Seems to be very attracted by parts or details of objects.") and *(IV) Health* (25 items, e.g. "Unaware of body sensations such as hunger, hot, cold, need to use toilet.") (appendix D). To detect possible small improvements during the time span of 8 weeks, the rating-scale was extended from three to five points (cp. Pineda et al., 2008) in the item sections *I, II* and *III,* ranging from "not true" to "very true". The items in section *IV* needed to be rated on a four point scale, ranging from "not a problem" to "serious problem". The severity of the disorder is indicated by higher scores of the subscales. For the statistical analyses of the present study, the questionnaires filled out by parents and teachers were separately included, as also done for the SRS-2. Furthermore, 'general' scores were created as well by calculating item values as the mean of both parent and teacher rating of the corresponding items. The original version of the ATEC (available online at no charge) was normed on the first 1,358 initial ATEC forms submitted to the Autism Research Institute (Rimland & Edelson, 2000). The internal consistency was high, the reported Pearson split-half coefficients ranged from .815 to .920 for the subscales and was .942 for the total score. At this time, data rating the test-retest reliability is not available, but initial analyses are in progress (ibid., 2005 Update). Regarding the validity, primary data is not available either, but publications are in preparation. However, the authors refer to other published studies that have shown "the ATEC to be sensitive to changes as a result of a treatment" (ibid.).

4.3.4 *Florida Apraxia Screening Test, Revised (FAST-R; modified)*

The FAST-R is a test to determine the performance of skilled motor gestures, originally developed to examine limb apraxia in patients with lateralized brain damage (Gonzales Rothi, Raymer, & Heilman, 1997). The gestures need to be shown as a reaction to a command, to an imitation or by utilizing an actual tool appropriately. This advantageous approach can be used to investigate if children with Autism Spectrum Disorder only show an imitation deficit, as described earlier, or if the performance of gestures is generally impaired (Mostofsky et al., 2006). Mostofsky et al. adapted the original version of the FAST-R to create a more child-appropriate test, only including gestures that were familiar to children. This adapted version was the basis for the present study, but some minor modifications were made. Single items were exchanged in order create a test more appropriate for the existing group of participants. The final test consisted of three parts, of which the first two were divided into two subtests each, demanding intransitive gestures as well as transitive gestures, which require the use of imagined objects (appendix E). The three main parts of the test measured the ability *(a) to follow a command by showing a verbally requested gesture* (24 items, 12 for each subtest; item examples: *intransitive*: “Show me how you clap your hands.”, *transitive*: “Show me how you use a comb to fix your hair.”), *(b) to imitate a shown gesture* (same 24 items as in (a), but gestures were only shown and needed to be imitated) and *(c) to demonstrate the use of an actual tool* (12 items, e.g. “Show me how you use this.” – object (e.g. toothbrush) was present). The scoring of the reactions was based on the approach of Gonzales Rothi et al. (1997), in the sense that gestures were rated as correct or incorrect, with different grading of the incorrect responses. However, the scoring key was simplified for this study in order to ease the rating process of the reactions. This simplification also happened with the goal of adapting the content of the test to the central question of the study, as the focus was not on differentiating various types of errors but on the development of a more accurate response over time due to improvements in the brain wave activity. Therefore the reactions were scored on a five point scale, ranging from a “correct response” to “no response”, with different gradations in between concerning the accuracy and target association of the reaction. An important advantage of this test is that it is suitable for both verbal and nonverbal children and therefore could be used to assess all children participating in the study. The inter-rater reliability for the child-adapted version (Mostofsky et al., 2006) was high, reported Pearson’s correlation coefficients were .86 for total percentage of correct responses and 0.93 for total absolute errors. Furthermore they found that children with an ASD had fewer total percent correct responses than the control group and made significantly more total errors as well as errors in all three subtests (ibid.).

5 Results

The following analyses were conducted in order to assess the effectiveness of the implemented Neurofeedback Training as an additional intervention for Autism Spectrum Disorders. Since the brain maps of the existing heterogeneous sample were very diverse and requested individual training protocols, QEEG data was initially analyzed as single cases. Subsequently, cases with similar target areas and frequencies were combined and their changes over time were analyzed with paired-samples t-tests. The SRS-2 scores were analyzed using a repeated measures MANOVA. Nonparametric tests were used to analyze the ATEC and the FAST-R. The alpha level for rejecting the null hypothesis was set at p equal to or less than .05. Missing data was replaced separately for each questionnaire, using two different methods as described later. A maximum of two missing values per variable (<15%) was permitted. In cases of more than two missing values, the variable was excluded from further analyses. All analyses were conducted with the program *IBM SPSS Statistics 20* (IBM Corporation, 2011). Appendix G displays a correlation matrix containing the participants' gender and age as well as all subscales of the two questionnaires and the imitation test.

5.1 QEEG

As stated earlier, individual training protocols were required due to very heterogeneous brain maps that displayed abnormalities in different areas. For this reason, it was not reasonable to compare the treatment and control group as a whole as there were no common values that could have been related to each other meaningfully. In addition, important information on inter-individual differences in the brain wave activity would have been disregarded. In order to capture all individual characteristics and changes over time, all subjects were analyzed as single cases (Köhler, 2008). First, a 'deviation score' was generated for each frequency band by averaging the given z-scores for each electrode position. Table 3 shows the deviation scores of the absolute power for each participant and frequency band separately. Table 4 contains the correspondent deviation scores of the relative power. The scores of both brain maps of each child are displayed, revealing the deviation at the beginning and the end of the study. All abnormalities were rated in their severity and classified as small ($-1 < z < 1$), medium ($1 \leq z < 2$ or $-2 < z \leq -1$) or large ($z \leq -2$ or $z \geq 2$) deviations. All changes over time were then assessed concerning their direction. These changes were not calculated statistically, but were evaluated regarding their clinical importance. If the correspondent z-value at t2 was classified into another deviation category, this was rated as a positive or negative change over time.

At the time of the pre-assessment, four children in the control group showed mainly small deviations concerning all recorded categories. Due to this imbalanced initial situation, a direct comparison to the individuals of the treatment group was not reasonable at this point. Therefore the subsequent analyses will focus on the subjects within the treatment group. However, some children of the control group revealed higher deviations at the time of the post-assessments that were not recognizable in the first brain map. A few of these important changes will be referred to later.

Table 3: Deviation scores (average z-scores) of each frequency band regarding the Absolute Power and classification of the severity of the deviation[1]. The column 'change' displays the 'importance' of a change[2] in terms of the movement to a severity category closer to the final target value of $z = 0$.

Group	Subject ID	Delta t1	Delta t2	Delta change	Theta t1	Theta t2	Theta change	Alpha t1	Alpha t2	Alpha change	Beta t1	Beta t2	Beta change	High Beta t1	High Beta t2	High Beta change
Treatment Group	01	-1.10 medium	-0.43 small	+	-1.06 medium	-0.86 small	+	-1.44 medium	-1.19 medium	o	0.38 small	0.23 small	o	2.32 large	1.62 medium	+
	02	2.42 large	0.46 small	++	0.59 small	0.29 small	o	-0.66 small	-0.51 small	o	0.36 small	0.30 small	o	0.92 small	0.67 small	o
	03	-0.53 small	-0.04 small	o	-0.49 small	0.03 small	o	-1.12 medium	-1.06 medium	o	-0.36 small	-0.46 small	o	0.61 small	0.31 small	o
	04	-0.18 small	-0.12 small	o	-0.22 small	0.04 small	o	-0.91 small	-1.03 medium	-	-0.05 small	-0.47 small	o	0.89 small	0.01 small	o
	05	1.73 medium	1.79 medium	o	0.98 small	1.13 medium	-	0.21 small	0.96 small	o	1.03 medium	1.28 medium	o	2.20 large	1.77 medium	+
	06	0.81 small	-0.25 small	o	-0.19 small	-0.35 small	o	-1.10 medium	-1.06 medium	o	0.52 small	1.52 medium	-	-0.21 small	0.27 small	o
	07	2.10 large	0.22 small	++	1.04 medium	0.09 small	+	1.65 medium	0.69 small	+	1.80 medium	0.98 small	+	1.81 medium	0.53 small	+
	09	1.66 medium	0.82 small	+	0.72 small	0.20 small	o	0.58 small	-1.09 medium	-	-0.06 small	-0.73 small	o	0.12 small	0.50 small	o
Control Group	08	0.86 small	1.78 medium	-	1.10 medium	0.60 small	+	0.73 small	0.16 small	o	0.64 small	0.05 small	o	0.26 small	-0.14 small	o
	10	-0.84 small	1.56 medium	-	-0.69 small	0.27 small	o	-1.56 medium	-0.93 small	+	-0.22 small	-0.43 small	o	0.85 small	1.19 medium	-
	11	-0.29 small	0.91 small	o	-0.16 small	-0.04 small	o	-0.55 small	-0.40 small	o	0.49 small	0.89 small	o	0.72 small	0.91 small	o
	12	-0.16 small	0.87 small	o	-0.19 small	0.88 small	o	-0.81 small	-0.27 small	o	0.12 small	0.36 small	o	0.53 small	0.92 small	o
	14	-0.30 small	2.20 large	- -	-0.77 small	0.18 small	o	-1.51 medium	-0.93 small	+	-0.63 small	-0.06 small	o	0.42 small	0.80 small	o
	15	0.83 small	0.63 small	o	0.59 small	0.71 small	o	-0.13 small	-0.09 small	o	0.88 small	0.67 small	o	1.73 medium	1.24 medium	o

[1] Deviations: small: $-1 < z < 1$; medium: $1 \leq z < 2$ or $-2 < z \leq -1$; large: $z \leq -2$ or $z \geq 2$

[2] Change over time:
+ + shift of 2 categories closer to the target value ('large' to 'small' deviation)
\+ shift of 1 category closer to the target value ('large' to 'medium' deviation; 'medium' to 'small' deviation)
o no shift in category
\- shift of 1 category further away from the target value ('small' to 'medium' deviation; 'medium' to 'large' deviation)
\- - shift of 2 categories further away from the target value ('small' to 'large')

Table 4: Deviation scores (average z-scores) of each frequency band regarding the **Relative Power** and classification of the severity of the deviation[1]. The column 'change' displays the 'importance' of a change[2] in terms of the movement to a severity category closer to the final target value of $z = 0$.

Group	Subject ID	Delta t1	Delta t2	Delta change	Theta t1	Theta t2	Theta change	Alpha t1	Alpha t2	Alpha change	Beta t1	Beta t2	Beta change	High Beta t1	High Beta t2	High Beta change
Treatment Group	01	-0.09 small	0.61 small	o	-0.66 small	-0.59 small	o	-1.73 medium	-1.47 medium	o	1.69 medium	1.26 medium	o	2.72 large	2.02 large	o
	02	2.09 large	0.67 small	+ +	-0.26 small	0.53 small	o	-2.41 large	-1.05 medium	+	-0.43 small	0.43 small	o	0.22 small	0.62 small	o
	03	0.70 small	0.90 small	o	0.28 small	0.83 small	o	-0.91 small	-1.27 medium	-	0.53 small	-0.02 small	o	1.19 medium	0.78 small	+
	04	0.61 small	0.82 small	o	0.23 small	0.87 small	o	-1.03 medium	-1.21 medium	o	0.60 small	-0.08 small	o	1.28 medium	0.54 small	+
	05	0.82 small	0.49 small	o	0.17 small	0.04 small	o	-1.00 medium	-0.16 small	+	0.19 small	0.24 small	o	1.11 medium	0.59 small	+
	06	1.44 medium	0.03 small	+	-0.47 small	-0.27 small	o	-1.76 medium	-1.19 medium	o	0.68 small	2.24 large	- -	-0.19 small	0.53 small	o
	07	0.51 small	-0.17 small	o	-0.54 small	-0.26 small	o	0.42 small	0.57 small	o	0.33 small	0.81 small	o	0.30 small	0.30 small	o
	09	1.47 medium	1.45 medium	o	0.10 small	0.50 small	o	-0.63 small	-2.01 large	- -	-0.93 small	-0.67 small	o	-0.72 small	0.68 small	o
Control Group	08	-0.01 small	1.52 medium	-	0.75 small	-0.13 small	o	0.09 small	-0.74 small	o	-0.03 small	-0.72 small	o	-0.23 small	-0.63 small	o
	10	0.54 small	1.85 medium	-	0.19 small	-0.19 small	o	-1.42 medium	-2.02 large	-	1.03 medium	-0.89 small	+	1.65 medium	0.83 small	+
	11	0.12 small	1.04 medium	-	0.05 small	-0.62 small	o	-0.53 small	-0.97 small	o	0.99 small	0.78 small	o	0.96 small	0.68 small	o
	12	0.46 small	0.49 small	o	0.19 small	0.93 small	o	-0.91 small	-1.17 medium	-	0.70 small	0.00 small	o	0.92 small	0.62 small	o
	14	1.38 medium	2.42 large	-	0.06 small	-0.82 small	o	-1.79 medium	-2.62 large	-	0.36 small	-1.05 medium	-	1.32 medium	0.19 small	+
	15	0.35 small	0.22 small	o	0.23 small	0.64 small	o	-0.76 small	-0.59 small	o	0.72 small	0.54 small	o	1.06 medium	0.83 medium	+

[1] Deviations: small: $-1 < z < 1$; medium: $1 \leq z < 2$ or $-2 < z \leq -1$; large: $z \leq -2$ or $z \geq 2$

[2] Change over time: + + shift of 2 categories closer to the target value ('large' to 'small' deviation)
+ shift of 1 category closer to the target value ('large' to 'medium' deviation; 'medium' to 'small' deviation)
o no shift in category
- shift of 1 category further away from the target value ('small' to 'medium' deviation; 'medium' to 'large' deviation)
- - shift of 2 categories further away from the target value ('small' to 'large')

Although the training protocols were individualized for each child, some similar abnormal characteristics were found in several children of the treatment group. Those cases were combined for more detailed analyses. It should be noted that the subjects were not grouped by their complete protocols. For each particular frequency band and power dimension, the children selected showed comparable medium or large deviations, and therefore had the same targets set as part of their protocol. In almost all cases, participants had more than one target due to several abnormalities in the brain wave activity. For this reason, each subject was included more than once in the following examinations. However, not all training targets are shown here as several abnormalities only appeared in single individuals and a detailed examination of each individual protocol was not feasible within this paper. Table 5 displays important target frequency bands and the relevant electrode positions that showed essential deviations. All participants of the treatment group that showed these abnormalities are listed. Means and standard deviations of each subgroup are given for the pre- and post-recordings. The *t*- and *p*-values of paired-samples t-tests indicate if the change over time was significant for the particular subgroups. The respective average deviation scores of each individual were recalculated for these analyses, only including z-scores of the designated electrodes. Since the number of individuals in those subgroups was very small, the alpha level was set at $p \leq .10$ for the t-tests. In this case, significant results would still indicate clinically important changes in the brain wave activity.

Table 5: Training targets for several subjects in the treatment group and means of the pre-and post-QEEG recordings as well as results of paired-sample t-tests

Subject IDs	**Frequency band and power dimension**	**Designated electrode positions**	t1(pre) *M* (*SD*)	t2 (post) *M* (*SD*)	***t***	***p*** *(2-tailed)*	***d***
2,5, 7,9	Delta (1-4 Hz), Absolute Power	all 19	1.98 (0.35)	0.82 (0.69)	2.418	.094*	1.21
3,4, 6	Alpha (8-12 Hz), Absolute Power	central: C_3, C_4, C_Z; parietal: P_3, P_4, P_Z; occipital: O_1, O_2	-1.39 (0.17)	-1.45 (0.16)	2.521	.128	-.15
1,2, 6	Alpha (8-12 Hz), Relative Power	all 19	-1.97 (0.38)	-1.23 (0.22)	-2.230	.156	-1.29
1,5, 7	High Beta (25-30 Hz), Absolute Power	frontal: F_3, F_7, F_4, F_8, F_Z; central: C_3, C_4, C_Z; parietal: P_3, P_4, P_Z; occipital: O_1, O_2; temporal: T_3, T_5, T_4, T_6	2.30 (0.28)	1.39 (0.65)	3.879	.060*	2.24
3,4, 5	High Beta (25-30 Hz), Relative Power	central: C_3, C_4, C_Z; parietal: P_3, P_4, P_Z	2.14 (0.22)	1.52 (0.32)	4.597	.044**	2.56

Note: *M* = mean, *SD* = standard deviation.
* $p \leq .10$.
** $p \leq .05$.

One-sample Shapiro-Wilk tests showed that the data did not deviate significantly ($p \leq .05$) from normality (appendix H). Results of a paired-samples t-test showed that participants were able to successfully reduce excessive delta waves during the training period, $t(3) = 2.418$, $p \leq .10$. In addition, the data revealed that training participants could neither significantly increase the absolute nor the relative alpha power towards normality. Individuals, whose brain maps initially displayed excessive absolute or relative High Beta power, were both able to significantly reduce the over-arousal, $t(2) = 3.879$, $p \leq .10$, or increased presence of this frequency band towards normality, $t(2) = 4.597$, $p \leq .05$. Effect sizes of the significant results ranged from $d = 1.21$ to 2.56. Besides mainly positive transformations, it should be noted that the post-brain maps also revealed some isolated worsening of previously not affected frequencies and areas. Changes from a small to a large deviation were observed for the relative beta power of subject 6 as well as for the relative alpha power of subject 9 (see table 4 for details). However, the data clearly displays that all members of the treatment group mainly achieved improvements in the targeted brain wave activity over time.

5.2 Social Responsiveness Scale (SRS-2)

The SRS-2 total score as well as the two subscales *RRB (Restricted Interests and Repetitive Behavior)* and *SCI (Social Communication and Interaction)* were considered. Missing data was replaced with the median value of the certain items in the norm sample (Constantino & Gruber, 2012). Results of a one-sample Kolmogorov-Smirnov test showed that questionnaire data did not deviate significantly from normality (appendix H). At the time of the pre-assessment, the treatment and control group showed no significant differences at any scale, $F(4,11) = .087$, $p = .985$, $\eta_p^2 = .031$. To examine if all participants improved over time (*H1*) and if the post-ratings of the children in the treatment group were significantly better than in the control group (*H3*), a 2 (time: pre vs. post) × 2 (group: treatment vs. control) repeated measures MANOVA was conducted. Table 6 displays the means and standard deviations of the total scores as well as the two sub scores and additionally the same scores separated for parent ratings and teacher ratings. Higher scores indicate higher impairments and severity of the disorder. Also shown are the corresponding *p*-values of main effects of time as well as univariate time (2) × group (2) interactions.

The multivariate analysis revealed a main effect of time, $F(2,13) = 6.881$, $p < .01$, $\eta_p^2 = .514$, but no interaction effect was found, $F(2,13) = 1.340$, $p = .296$, $\eta_p^2 = .171$. When the data was examined separately, neither a main effect of time, $F(2,13) = 2.834$, $p = .095$, $\eta_p^2 = .304$, nor an interaction effect, $F(2,13) = .337$, $p = .720$, $\eta_p^2 = .049$, were found for the parent ratings. Analysis of the teacher ratings showed a main effect of time, $F(2,13) = 4.915$, $p < .05$, $\eta_p^2 = .431$, but also no interaction effect, $F(2,13) = 1.314$, $p = .302$, $\eta_p^2 = .168$, was found.

Table 6: Means and standard deviations of the SRS-2 total score and sub scores for the treatment and the control group as well as p-values and η_p^2-values of the main effects of time and time × group interactions

	Treatment group		Control group					
	t1(pre) *M (SD)*	t2 (post) *M (SD)*	t1 (pre) *M (SD)*	t2 (post) *M (SD)*	p *time*	η_p^2	p *time × group*	η_p^2
SRS-2 total score	110.44 (11.91)	89.38 (20.25)	104.06 (30.93)	96.06 (37.32)	.003**	.471	.135	.152
SCI	89.06 (9.10)	72.94 (16.07)	83.75 (25.73)	77.69 (31.53)	.006**	.429	.163	.134
RRB	21.38 (3.70)	16.44 (4.87)	20.31 (5.60)	18.38 (6.74)	.002**	.502	.123	.161
SRS-2 total score parents	110.75 (22.95)	95.50 (25.43) [a]	106.63 (25.05)	99.25 (34.45)	.067	.220	.500	.033
SCI parents	87.75 (17.95)	77.13 (18.22) [a]	84.63 (21.90)	79.50 (28.82)	.102	.180	.551	.026
RRB parents	23.00 (6.46)	18.38 (7.56) [a]	22.00 (5.24)	19.75 (7.96)	.028*	.299	.413	.048
SRS-2 total score teachers	110.13 (20.15)	83.25 (25.06) [b]	101.50 (44.73)	92.88 (42.96)	.007**	.420	.124	.160
SCI teachers	90.38 (16.69)	68.75 (21.17) [b]	82.88 (36.93)	75.88 (35.00)	.010*	.385	.153	.140
RRB teachers	19.75 (5.95)	14.50 (4.34) [b]	18.63 (8.07)	17.00 (7.62)	.024*	.314	.203	.113

Note: *M* = mean, *SD* = standard deviation.
* $p \leq .05$.
** $p \leq .01$.
[a] Effect of time within treatment group is marginally significant ($p < .10$).
[b] Effect of time within treatment group is significant ($p < .05$).

Within the treatment group, the parent and teacher ratings were also analyzed separately, in order to examine whether both respondents perceived a change (*H5* and *H6*). A 2 (time: pre vs. post) × 1 (group) repeated measures MANOVA was conducted for parent ratings and for teacher ratings. No significant change over time was found for the parent assessments, $F(2,6) = 2.291$, $p = .182$, $\eta_p^2 = .433$. Univariate analyses revealed marginally significant improvements ($p < .10$) over time for the total score and both subscales (appendix I). Regarding the teacher assessments, multivariate analysis showed a marginally significant change over time, $F(2,6) = 3.984$, $p = .079$, $\eta_p^2 = .570$. However, univariate analyses displayed significant results ($p < .05$) for the total score and both subscales. To investigate whether the assessments of the children in the treatment group by their parents differed from those by their teachers at t2 (*H7*), a paired samples t-test was conducted. No significant differences in the two assessments were found in the SRS-2 total score, $t(7) = 1{,}149$, $p = .288$, $d = .406$, or in the two subscales SCI and RRB, $t(7) = 1{,}031$, $p = .337$, $d = .365$; $t(7) = 1{,}452$; $p = .190$, $d = .514$.

5.3 Autism Treatment Evaluation Checklist (ATEC, modified)

All four subscales were used for the following analyses. Missing item values were replaced with the series mean of the correspondent item, when necessary. However, 6 items had to be excluded due to too many missing values (>15%). For this reason the subscale *IV Health* was included in the analyses with only 19 items, instead of the intended 25 items. For the subscale *I Language and Communication* only 13 participants were included in the subsequent analyses as 3 children were non-verbal and inclusion of their scores would have biased the results distinctly. For this reason, no ATEC total score (as the sum of all sub scores) was calculated, since only 13 participants could have been considered as well. This was also in order to keep the results as comparable as possible and to simplify the interpretation of the resulting scores. Results of a one-sample Kolmogorov-Smirnov test and of a Levene's test of equality of error variances revealed some significant results, thus the premises for parametric tests were violated (appendix H).

Wilcoxon Signed Rank Tests were conducted for each group separately, in order to investigate if all participants improved over time and therefore had lower ratings in the post-test (*H1*). Table 7 displays the median values of all subscales as well as the *Z*- and *p*-values of the pre-post-assessments in each group and the corresponding effect sizes *r*. Regarding the treatment group, ratings on all ATEC subscales were significantly lower after the training. The parent and teacher ratings, considered separately (*H5* and *H6*), both revealed significantly lower evaluations in three out of four subscales respectively. In the control group, only one subscale value in each examination revealed significant reductions in the ratings over time. Effect sizes of the significant changes ranged from $r = -.69$ to $-.89$. To examine whether the parent and teacher ratings in the treatment group differed from each other at t2 (*H7*), an additional Wilcoxon Signed Rank Test was conducted (appendix J). The median values of the teacher and parent assessments did not differ from each other at t1 ($p > .05$). At t2 only the teacher rating on subscale *IV Health* ($Md = 6.50$) was significantly lower than the parent rating ($Md = 12.50$), $z = -2.106$, $p < .05$, $r = -.75$. All other parent and teacher subscale ratings did not differ significantly from each other in the post-assessment.

Table 7: Median values for all ATEC subscales for the treatment and control group and Z- and p-values for the comparison of pre- and post-assessments within each group as well as the corresponding effect sizes r

	Treatment group					**Control group**				
	t1(pre) *Md*	t2 (post) *Md*	*Z*	***p*** ***(2-tailed)***	***r***	t1 (pre) *Md*	t2 (post) *Md*	*Z*	***p*** ***(2-tailed)***	***r***
ATEC										
I Lang. & Comm.	28.25	19.75	-2.38	.017*	-.84	16.60	10.50	-1.75	.080	-.78
II Sociab. & Interact.	37.75	28.75	-2.52	.012*	-.89	39.00	33.75	-2.24	.025*	-.79
III Behav. & Interests	45.75	36.07	-2.52	.012*	-.89	50.25	46.80	-.70	.483	-.25
IV Health	14.50	9.75	-2.52	.012*	-.89	15.25	17.25	-.21	.833	-.07
ATEC (parents)										
I Lang. & Comm.	27.00	20.50	-2.10	.035*	-.74	19.00	13.20	-.67	.500	-.30
II Sociab. & Interact.	39.50	28.33	-2.39	.017*	-.84	41.23	35.00	-2.24	.025*	-.79
III Behav. & Interests	42.00	35.50	-2.52	.012*	-.89	46.80	47.00	-.42	.672	-.15
IV Health	15.00	12.50 [c]	-1.41	.159	-.49	17.00	17.00	-.21	.833	-.07
ATEC (teachers)										
I Lang. & Comm.	28.50	20.00	-2.37	.018*	-.84	15.20	10.00	-2.02	.043*	-.90
II Sociab. & Interact.	39.50	30.00	-1.68	.092	-.60	38.00	41.00	-1.27	.204	-.45
III Behav. & Interests	44.91	37.63	-1.96	.050*	-.69	52.50	41.10	-.35	.726	-.12
IV Health	14.50	6.50 [c]	-2.52	.012*	-.89	14.00	15.50	-.17	.866	-.06

Note: * $p \leq .05$. [c] The teacher rating in the treatment group at t2 is significantly lower than the parent rating ($p < .05$).

Mann-Whitney U Tests were conducted in order to examine if the improvements over time were significantly higher in the treatment group than in the control group (*H3*). Table 8 displays the difference values for each subtest and the corresponding *p*-values and effect sizes *r*. Higher difference values indicate a larger decrease in the ratings. It appeared that the treatment group showed a significantly larger difference in their pre- and post-assessments than the control group (indicating improvement) on the subscales *III* and *IV*. The pre-post-difference of the parent ratings on the subscale *III Behavior and Interests* was significantly higher in the treatment than in the control group, whereas this applies to the teacher ratings on subscale *IV Health*. Effect sizes of the significant differences ranged from $r = -.53$ to $-.63$.

Table 8: Difference values (indicating changes from pre- to post-test) of all ATEC subscales for the treatment and the control group; as well as U-, Z- and p-values for the comparison of both groups

	Treatment group		Control group		*U*	*Z*	*p*	*r*
Difference values	Range (min – max)	Md	Range (min – max)	Md			*(2-tailed)*	
ATEC								
I Lang. & Comm.	-0.1 – 10	4.4	-1 – 8	4.5	16.0	-.586	.558	-.15
II Sociab. & Interact.	3 – 27	8.8	-3 – 21	7.3	27.5	-.473	.636	-.12
III Behav. & Interests	2 – 19.5	7.5	-7 – 7.5	0.4	10.5	-2.261	.024*	-.57
IV Health	1.5 – 12	3.8	-5.7 – 4.5	0	12.0	-2.104	.035*	-.53
ATEC (parents)								
I Lang. & Comm.	-2.2 – 7	4	-8 – 7	4.8	18.0	-.295	.768	-.07
II Sociab. & Interact.	-1 – 21	15	-7 – 22.5	11.5	31.5	-.053	.958	-.01
III Behav. & Interests	1 – 21	9.5	-11.4 – 10	1	10.0	-2.317	.020*	-.58
IV Health	-3 – 10	2.5	-10 – 10	0.45	27.5	-.474	.636	-.12
ATEC (teachers)								
I Lang. & Comm.	0 – 13	7.5	1 – 15	5.2	18.5	-.220	.826	-.06
II Sociab. & Interact.	-6 – 38.1	4.6	-6 – 29	2.5	28.5	-.368	.713	-.09
III Behav. & Interests	-7 – 24.6	8	-5 – 21	0	20.0	-1.260	.208	-.32
IV Health	2 – 17.1	8.3	-10 – 6.1	0.5	8.0	-2.528	.011*	-.63

Note: The difference values resulted from the calculation: subscale score at t1 minus subscale score at t2. Therefore positive difference values indicate improvements over time as the ratings of the post-test assessment were lower (indicating less impairment).

* $p \leq .05$.

5.4 Florida Apraxia Screening Test, Revised (FAST-R; modified)

To examine the improvement in imitation abilities, the total score as well as all sub scores of the three different test parts were considered. Results of a one-sample Kolmogorov-Smirnov test displayed that the data deviated significantly from normality hence premises for parametric tests were not given (appendix H).

In order to investigate if all participants improved over time and therefore received higher ratings for their gesture accuracy (*H1*), a Wilcoxon Signed Rank Test was conducted for each group (appendix K). Participants in the treatment group improved significantly ($p \leq .05$) in all domains, except in one subtest (*transitive gesture to command*). Effect sizes of the significant changes ranged from $r = -.69$ to $-.90$. Participants in the control group improved significantly ($p \leq .05$) in all subtests of part (a) (*transitive gesture to command, intransitive gesture to command and total score for gesture to command*) and in the FAST-R total score, but did not show any significant changes in the remaining parts of the test. Effect sizes of the significant changes ranged from $r = -.69$ to $-.89$.

To analyze if the improvements over time were significantly higher in the treatment group than in the control group (*H4*), a Mann-Whitney U Test was conducted. Table 9 displays the difference values for each test part, which represent the changes over time in the accuracy of the gestures. Higher difference values indicate greater improvements in the shown gestures. In all tests, but one, the two groups did not differ significantly in their extent of improvement. Only in the third test part (*gesture with tool use*) did children of the treatment group show a significantly greater improvement than the control group ($r = .51$).

Table 9: Difference values (indicating changes from pre- to post-test) of all FAST-R sub scores and the total score for the treatment and the control group; as well as U-, Z- and p-values for the comparison of both groups and corresponding effect sizes r.

Difference values	Treatment group Range (min – max)	Treatment group Md	Control group Range (min – max)	Control group Md	*U*	*Z*	*p* (*2-tailed*)	*r*
(a) Gesture to command								
intransitive	-3 – 31	5	-1 – 19	7	31.5	-.053	.958	-.01
transitive	-1 – 8	1	0 – 10	5	19.5	-1.366	.182	-.34
total	-4 – 31	10	1 – 27	9.5	31.5	-.053	.958	-.01
(b) Gesture to imitation								
intransitive	-1 – 18	2.5	-9 – 8	0	17.0	-1.586	.113	-.40
transitive	1 – 15	3	-8 – 8	1	17.0	-1.587	.113	-.40
total	2 – 33	6	-17 – 10	2.5	16.0	-1.685	.092	-.42
(c) Gesture with tool use	0 – 13	5.5	-3 – 8	0.5	12.5	-2.059	.040*	-.51
FAST-R total score	7 – 73	18	-13 – 37	13	22.0	-1.051	.293	-.26

Note: Higher difference values indicate higher improvement of the performance over time.
* $p \leq .05$.

6 Discussion

The present study reveals important findings concerning the effectiveness of Neurofeedback training for Autism Spectrum Disorders as an additional intervention. Considerable improvements have been detected that turn this paper into a contribution to the currently growing field of research for effective treatments for ASD.

As stated earlier, the QEEG recordings were hardly directly comparable between all individuals. Most children in the control group revealed generally less abnormalities during the first recordings than the treatment group. However, the brain maps of the post-recordings showed that the brain wave activity of the subjects in the control group mainly remained similar and only partly improved in a few cases. Interestingly several children exhibited distinct abnormalities only in the second brain map. For example, three children of the control group showed clearly increased absolute delta power above normality that was not noticeable in the first brain maps. An explicit decrease of relative alpha power was also observable in three children only at the time of the second recording. These findings do not indicate an improvement in brain wave activity over time without a neurological treatment (*H1*). On the contrary, participants of the treatment group revealed clinically important improvements in at least one individual training target, identifiable with distinct decreases in the z-scores (*H1* and *H2*). Focusing on the treatment group, children who received Neurofeedback training showed more abnormalities in their initial brain maps than the control group. Although the brain maps were individually different, some patterns could be found in several children and go along with previous findings of other researchers. In a review on resting state EEG abnormalities in ASD, Wang et al. (2013) stated that in several studies excessive power was found in low-frequency and high-frequency bands, while reduced power was observed in the middle-range frequency band alpha. Significantly less alpha power and an increased power of low-frequency bands often correspond with observable cognitive impairments (Klimesch, 1999). Similar abnormality patterns were found in the present study. Most children who received a Neurofeedback training exclusively improved their brain wave activity successfully, which is consistent with the positive findings of the other assessment instruments. These developments clearly speak for the implementation of individualized training protocols (Thatcher, 2009) in order to achieve the greatest improvement possible for each participant.

According to the ratings on the Social Responsiveness Scale (SRS-2) all participants achieved a reduction in their autistic and related symptoms over time from pre-intervention to post-intervention (*H1*). However, no interaction effect was found, indicating that individuals who received an additional Neurofeedback training did not achieve significantly greater improvements than the control group (*H3*). Within the treatment group, parents and teachers reported improvements following the training (*H5* and *H6*). The ratings of the different respondents did not significantly differ from each other (*H7*). The reason for the similarly existing improvement of the control group may be found in the research design. The children in the control group also received a basic treatment they may have benefitted from and therefore accomplished a comparable therapy progress. This clearly highlights the effectiveness of the basic comprehensive treatment that is implemented at the therapy center.

The ratings on the Autism Treatment Evaluation Checklist (ATEC) showed similar positive results for the treatment group, indicating that these participants successfully reduced autistic mannerisms and related abnormalities, whereas the control group improved only in the domain of *sociability and interaction* (*H1*). These findings are more in line with previous studies that often stated improvements only in the treatment group, compared to no changes in the control group (e.g. Jarusiewicz, 2002; Kouijzer et al., 2010). In a direct comparison of the post-assessments, the treatment group achieved greater improvements than the control group regarding the ratings of their *health* situation as well as their *behavior and interests* (*H3*). Within the treatment group, both parents and teachers reported improvements in three out of four domains (*H5 and H6*) and none of the evaluations differed significantly between the two groups (*H7*). Teachers' ratings were only better than the parent ratings regarding the children's *health* constitution, but this result should be interpreted with caution, as teachers may also only have restricted knowledge of specific somatic conditions due to the limited time they spend with the children at the therapy center. However, in all other domains, which mainly refer to communication, interaction and behavior, the ratings of the parents and teachers did not differ significantly. This novel conclusion, identified with both questionnaires, might be a basis for further investigations as it shows an important potential benefit of Neurofeedback training. The results can be an indicator for effects of generalization, in the sense that the children are able to transfer their positive behavioral and communicational training effects to other environmental contexts.

In the imitation test (FAST-R), it was challenging for numerous participants to follow the different instructions correctly. On the other hand, it should be noted, that some participants did not show any problems in imitating gestures or following verbal commands that required a gestural reaction. Children with impaired abilities showed observable difficulties in all subtests. The most challenging task for these children was to follow a verbal command and especially to imagine an object that they had to include in their reaction (*transitive gesture*). These findings go in line with those of Mostofsky et al. (2006), supporting the idea that children with an ASD often show a general deficit in the performance of gestures rather than only in imitation abilities. The treatment group was able to improve their performance significantly in almost all sub tests, while the control group only improved their *gestural reactions following verbal instructions* (*H1*). In the direct comparison of the performances at the end of the study, the treatment group only showed significantly greater improvements than the control group in the *demonstration of actual tool usage* (*H4*). Taking all results into account, Neurofeedback training might be related to the improvement of the gestural performance and thus could be potentially effective to increase higher neurocognitive abilities as well. However, the change of these basic abilities required for the FAST-R will need to be observed over longer time periods in subsequent studies in order to identify clear trends and actual cause-and-effect relations.

Summing up these findings, all participants revealed improvements in several domains over a relatively short period of time, which underlines the high quality and successful implementation of the comprehensive neurodevelopmental therapy approach at the Jacob's Ladder Center. Furthermore, the partly existing greater improvements and successful reduction of autistic symptoms of the treatment group compared to the control group provide initial endorsement for considering Neurofeedback training as an additional treatment element in order to possibly enhance basic treatment effects.

Besides important advantageous and novel aspects regarding the implementation, the study reveals several limitations that should not be disregarded as they include important suggestions for further research projects. Due to the small sample size and the special condition for the control group, conclusions are limited to similar treatment contexts. Participants were not assigned to the groups randomly, but based on the decision of the parents if they wanted an extra Neurofeedback training for their children. For this reason, the subjects were not totally comparable in all characteristic traits at the beginning of the study, which complicates the interpretation of the findings. It also should be mentioned that the parents were obligated to pay for the Neurofeedback sessions hence it is possible that they were prone to report significant changes as they might have expected to see improvements. The teachers were not blind to the treatment conditions either due to organizational aspects, thus unconscious expectancy effects could have affected their ratings. To guarantee the feasibility of the research project, only 15 training sessions were initially implemented, which is a relatively small amount compared to other studies and therefore could limit possible changes in the brain wave activity. A higher number of sessions often facilitates the detection of distinct reductions in abnormalities. Regarding the questionnaires, it is possible, that single items were understood variously by the different respondents which could have also led to distortions of the results. In some cases, the recording of the QEEG data was challenging due to partly disruptive behaviors or sensory issues of the participants. Therefore detectable abnormalities in the brain maps could also be attributed to inaccurate recordings rather than existing deviations in the brain wave activity. Additionally, brain maps in general display neuronal activity at only a certain point of time and thus can be fault-prone due to external circumstances and momentary individual physical and mental conditions. For this reason QEEG recording always should be interpreted carefully, especially when impaired individuals are involved.

In future research, the aforementioned weaknesses should be considered in order to enhance the validity of the results. Furthermore, future examinations should focus on the underlying processes of Neurofeedback training, in order to investigate if positive outcomes result from actual changes in the brain wave activity. It is for example also possible that improvements arise from an increased amount of attention that the children receive due to the training sessions. This could eventually affect the interactional and social skills of the individuals. Another aspect that should be focused on in future studies are the particular symptoms that can be reduced with the help of Neurofeedback training. In a recently published review, Holtmann et al. (2011) reported that Neurofeedback training often alleviated comorbid ADHD symptoms rather than distinct ADS symptoms. Therefore investigation is needed to examine which particular individuals on the autistic spectrum can benefit best from Neurofeedback training. An optimization of the Neurofeedback training itself could also enhance training effects. The LORETA z-score is an important development concerning this matter as certain brain areas can be identified and trained more accurately (Congedo et al., 2004).

This discussion clearly states that future research investigations need to be expanded to explicitly confirm Neurofeedback training as an effective treatment approach for Autism Spectrum Disorders. However, existing studies reveal promising results and this paper can be seen as a contribution to this developing research field.

References

Abarbanel, A. (1995). Gates, States, Rhythms, and Resonances: The Scientific Basis of Neurofeedback Training. *Journal of Neurotherapy*, *1*(2), 15–38.

American Psychiatric Association (2000). *Diagnostic and Statistical Manual of Mental Disorders, 4th Edition, Text Revision (DSM-IV-TR).* Arlington, Va: American Psychiatric Publishing, Incorporated.

American Psychiatric Association. (2013). *Diagnostic and Statistical Manual of Mental Disorders: DSM-5* (5th ed.). Arlington, Va: American Psychiatric Publishing, Incorporated.

American Psychiatric Association (2013b). *Autism Disorder Fact Sheet.* Retrieved from http://www.dsm5.org/Documents/Autism%20Spectrum%20Disorder%20Fact%20Sheet.pdf on 05/29/2013.

Arns, M., de Ridder, S., Strehl, U., Breteler, M., & Coenen, A. (2009). Efficacy of Neurofeedback Treatment in ADHD: the Effects on Inattention, Impulsivity and Hyperactivity: a Meta-Analysis. *Clinical EEG and Neuroscience, 40*(3), 180–189.

Autism Society (2013). *Facts and Statistics.* Retrieved from http://www.autism-society.org/about-autism/facts-and-statistics.html on 01/13/2014.

Autism Speaks (2013). *Facts about Autism.* Retrieved from http://www.autismspeaks.org/what-autism/facts-about-autism on 06/26/2013.

Billeci, L., Sicca, F., Maharatna, K., Apicella, F. Narzisi, A., Campatelli, G., …Muratori, F. (2013). On the Application of Quantitative EEG for Characterizing Autistic Brain: A Systematic Review. *Frontiers in Human Neuroscience, 7*, 1–15.

Bölte, S. (Hrsg.). (2009). *Autismus: Spektrum, Ursachen, Diagnostik, Intervention, Perspektiven.*Bern: Huber.

Bondy, A. S., & Frost, L. A. (1994). The Picture Exchange Communication System. *Focus on Autism and OtherDevelopmental Disabilities*, *9*(3), 1–19.

Coben, R., Linden, M., & Myers, T. E. (2010). Neurofeedback for Autistic Spectrum Disorder: A Review of the Literature. *Applied Psychophysiology and Biofeedback*, *35*(1), 83–105.

Coben, R., & Padolsky, I. (2007). Assessment-Guided Neurofeedback for Autistic Spectrum Disorder. *Journal of Neurotherapy*, *11*(1), 5–23.

Cochin, S., Barthelemy, C., Lejeune, B., Roux. S., & Martineau, J., (1998). Perception of motion and qEEG activity in human adults. *Electroencephalography and Clinical Neurophysiology, 107*(4), 287-295.

Congedo, M., Lubar, J. F., & Joffe, D. (2004). Low-Resolution Electromagnetic Tomography Neurofeedback. *IEEE Transactions on Neural Systems and Rehabilitation Engineering*, *12*(4), 387–397.

Constantino, J. N., & Gruber, C. P. (2012). *Social Responsiveness Scale, Second Edition (SRS-2)*. Torrance, CA: Western Psychological Services.

Dziobek, I., & Köhne, S. (2011). Bildgebung bei Autismusspektrumstörungen. *Der Nervenarzt, 82*(5), 564–572.

Frances, A. (2011). *The Autism Generation*. Retrieved from http://www.project-syndicate.org/commentary/the-autism-generation on 10/27/13.

Frazier, T. W., Youngstrom, E. A., Speer, L., Embacher, R., Law, P., Constantino, J., …Eng, C. (2012). Validation of Proposed DSM-5 Criteria for Autism Spectrum Disorder. *Journal of the American Academy of Child & Adolescent Psychiatry, 51*(1), 28–40.e3.

Gevensleben, H., Holl, B., Albrecht, B., Schlamp, D., Kratz, O., Studer, P., …Heinrich, H. (2009). Distinct EEG effects related to neurofeedback training in children with ADHD: A randomized controlled trial. *International Journal of Psychophysiology, 74*(2), 149–157

Gonzales Rothi, L. J., Raymer, A. M., & Heilman, K. M. (1997). Limb praxis assessment. In L. J.Gonzales Rothi & K.M. Heilman (Eds.), *Apraxia: The cognitive neuropsychology ofpraxis (pp. 61–73)*. Hove, UK: Psychology Press.

Holtmann, M., Steiner, S., Hohmann, S., Poustka, L., Banaschweski, T., & Bölte, S. (2011). Neurofeedback in autism spectrum disorders. *Developmental Medicine & Child Neurology, 53*(11), 986–993.

International Society for Neurofeedback and Research (2010). *Definition of Neurofeedback*. Retrieved from http://www.isnr.org/neurofeedback-info/learn-more-about-neurofeedback.cfm on 09/15/2013.

Jacob's Ladder Center (2013). *About Jacob's Ladder*. Retrieved from http://jacobsladder center.com/about-us/media/media-kit/ on 07/11/2013.

Jacob's Ladder Center (2013b). *Jacob's Ladder Methodology*. Retrieved from http://jacobsladdercenter.com/about-us/media/media-kit/on 7/11/2013.

Jarusiewicz, B. (2002). Efficacy of neurofeedback for children in the autistic spectrum: A pilot study. *Journal of Neurotherapy, 6*(4), 39–49.

Jasper, H. H. (1958). The ten-twenty electrode system of the International Federation. *Electroencephalography and Clinical Neurophysiology, 10*(2), 370–375.

Klimesch, W. (1999). EEG alpha and theta oscillations reflect cognitive and memory performance: a review and analysis. *Brain Research Reviews, 29*(2-3), 169–195.

Köhler, T. (2008). *Statistische Einzelfallanalyse: Eine Einführung mit Rechenbeispielen* (1. Aufl.). Weinheim, Basel: Beltz, PVU.

Kouijzer, M. E., de Moor, J. M., Gerrits, B. J., Congedo, M., & van Schie, H. T. (2009a). Neurofeedback improves executive functioning in children with autism spectrum disorders. *Research in Autism Spectrum Disorders, 3*(1), 145–162.

Kouijzer, M. E., de Moor, J. M., Gerrits, B. J., Buitelaar, J. K., & van Schie, H. T. (2009b). Long-term effects of neurofeedback treatment in autism. *Research in Autism Spectrum Disorders, 3*(2), 496–501.

Kouijzer, M. E., van Schie, H. T., de Moor, J. M., Gerrits, B. J., & Buitelaar, J. K. (2010). Neurofeedback treatment in autism. Preliminary findings in behavioral, cognitive, and neurophysiological functioning. *Research in Autism Spectrum Disorders, 4*(3), 386–399.

Larsen, S. (2012). *The neurofeedback solution: How to treat autism, ADHD, anxiety, brain injury,stroke, PTSD, and more*. Rochester, Vt: Healing Arts Press.

Lautenbacher, S., & Gauggel, S. (2010). *Neuropsychologie psychischer Störungen* (2. Aufl.). Berlin: Springer Medizin.

Lovaas, O. I. (1981). *Teaching Developmentally Disabled Children: The Me Book*. Austin, TX: Pro-Ed.

Lovaas, O. I. (1987). Behavioral treatment and normal educational and intellectual functioning in young autistic children. *Journal of Consulting and Clinical Psychology, 55,* 3–9.

Meyer-Lindenberg, A. (2011). Autismusspektrumstörungen. *Der Nervenarzt*, *82*(5), 551–552.

Mostofsky, S. H., Dubey, P., Jerath, V. K., Jansiewicz, E. M., Goldberg, M. C., & Denckla, M. B. (2006). Developmental dyspraxia is not limited to imitation in children with autism spectrum disorders. *Journal of the International Neuropsychological Society, 12*(3), 314–326.

Neurohealth Associates (2004). *The Science of Brainwaves. The Language of the Brain.* Retrieved from http://www.nhahealth.com/science.htm on 01/17/14.

Nickl-Jockschat, T., & Michel, T. (2011). Genetische und hirnstrukturelle Anomalien bei Autismus-Spektrum-Störungen. *Der Nervenarzt*, *82*(5), 618–627.

Niv, S. (2013). Clinical efficacy and potential mechanisms of neurofeedback. *Personality and Individual Differences*, *54*(6), 676–686.

Oberman, L. M., Hubbard, E. M., McCleery, J. P., Altschuler, E. L., Ramachandran, V. S., & Pineda, J. A. (2005). EEG evidence for mirror neuron dysfunction in autism spectrum disorders. *Cognitive Brain Research*, *24*(2), 190–198.

Pasco, G. (2010). Identification and Diagnosis of Autism Spectrum Disorders: An Update. *Pediatric Health*, *4*(1), 107–114.

Peniston, E. G., & Kulkosky, P. J. (1991). Alpha-Theta Brainwave Neuro-Feedback for Vietnam Veterans with Combat-related Post-Traumatic Stress Disorder. *Medical Psychotherapy, 4*, 47–60.

Perry, A. & Condillac, R. (2003). *Evidence-Based Practices for Children and Adolescents with Autism Spectrum Disorders: Review of the Literature and Practice Guidelines.* Toronto: Children's Mental Health Ontario.

Pineda, J., Brang, D., Hecht, E., Edwards, L., Carey, S., Bacon, M., …Rork, A. (2008). Positive behavioral and electrophysiological changes following neurofeedback training in children with autism. *Research in Autism Spectrum Disorders*, *2*(3), 557–581.

Pop-Jordanova, N., Zorcec, T., Demerdzieva, A., & Gucev, Z. (2010). QEEG characteristics and spectrum weighted frequency for children diagnosed as autistic spectrum disorder. *Nonlinear Biomedical Physics*, *4*(1), 4.

Poustka, F., Bölte, S., Feineis-Matthews, S. & Schmötzer, G. (2004). *Autistische Störungen. Leitfaden Kinder- und Jugendpsychotherapie.* Göttingen: Hogrefe.

Rimland, B., & Edelson, M. (1999). *Autism Treatment Evaluation Checklist (ATEC).* Autism Research Institute, San Diego, CA. Retrieved from http://www.autism.com/index.php/ind_atec on 05/10/2013.

Rimland, B., & Edelson, M. (2000). *Studies confirm validity of ATEC Report.* Retrieved from http://www.autism.com/ind_atec_report on 05/10/2013.

Rimland, B., & Edelson, M. (2005). *Studies confirm validity of ATEC Report – 2005 Update*. Retrieved from http://www.autism.com/ind_atec_report on 05/10/2013.

Rizzolatti, G., Fogassi, L., & Gallese, V. (2001). Neurophysiological mechanisms underlying the understanding and imitation of action. *Nature Reviews Neuroscience, 2*, 661–670.

Robbins, J. (2008). *A Symphony in the Brain: The Evolution of the New Brain Wave Biofeedback* (Rev. Ed.). New York: Grove Press.

Rogers, S. J., Hepburn, S. L., Stackhouse, T., & Wehner, E. (2003). Imitation performance in toddlers with autism and those with other developmental disorders. *Journal of Child Psychology and Psychiatry, 44*(5), 763–781.

Rutter, M. (2005). Incidence of autism spectrum disorders: Changes over time and their meaning. *Acta Paediatrica, 94*(1), 2–15.

Schopler, E., Mesibov, G. B., & Hearsey, K. A. (1995). Structured teaching in the TEACCH system. In E. Schopler & G. B. Mesibov (Eds.*), Learning and cognition in autism* (pp. 243-268). New York: Plenum.

Sinzig, J. (2011). *Frühkindlicher Autismus. Manuale psychischer Störungen bei Kindern und Jugendlichen*. Berlin, Heidelberg: Springer-Verlag Berlin Heidelberg.

Thatcher, R. W., Biver, C. J., North, D. M. (2007). Z Score EEG Biofeedback: Technical Foundations. Retrieved from http://www.appliedneuroscience.com/SurfaceZScoreNF.htm on 04/03/2013.

Thatcher, R. W. (2009). *Z TUNES: Nineteen Channel Quantitative EEG and EEG Biofeedback*. Retrieved from http://www.appliedneuroscience.com/SurfaceZScoreNF.htmon 04/03/ 2013.

Thatcher, R. W. (2010). Validity and Reliability of Quantitative Electroencephalography (qEEG). *Journal of Neurotherapy, 14*(2), 122–152.

Wang, J., Barstein, J., Ethridge, L. E., Mosconi, M. W., Takarae, Y., & Sweeney, J. A. (2013). Resting state EEG abnormalities in autism spectrum disorders. *Journal of Neurodevelopmental Disorders, 5*(1), 24.

Appendix

Appendix A: Information sheet about the project and consent form for participation

May 21, 2013

Dear Parents & Guardians,

We are planning on conducting a scientific research project during our summer school session and would like your child to participate in this project. We will scientifically monitor parts of our individual therapy programming and the implementation of Neurofeedback, in addition to our continuous supervision and evaluation of our individualized programs.

The focus group will be students diagnosed with Autism, Asperger's and Developmental Delays, between the ages of 3 - 18 years old.

During the research project, we will conduct 15 Neurofeedback sessions with your child and record 2 brain maps - before the first and after the last session.

Furthermore, we will be collecting data through program data, teacher questionnaires and parent questionnaires. As a parent, you will receive 2 questionnaires during the research project to assess different aspects of your child's behavior, cognition and emotional constitution.

The students will remain anonymous through reporting and will be referred to as a letter or number in the reporting.

In the event that you do not wish your child to have any Neurofeedback sessions, there still is a possibility to participate in the research project based on your child's daily therapy program at Jacob's Ladder. In this case there will be no additional costs for you.

If you are interested in participating in the research opportunity, please complete the second page of this letter and return to us on the first day of the summer program, Tuesday, 5/28/2013.

Please see the attached information sheet for a detailed description of the Neurofeedback process.

If you have any questions, please do not hesitate to contact us.

Sincerely,

Karla Brigiotta Director of Clinical Services	Franziska Eller Intern/Teacher

407 HARDSCRABBLE RD. ROSWELL, GA · 770.998.1017 · www.JACOBSLADDERCENTER.com

---

Student's Name: ______________________________

My child can participate in this research project: ___**YES** ___**NO**

If yes, please check one of the following options:

- ○ **We would like our child to receive Neurofeedback sessions in addition to the daily individual programming.**
- ○ **We would not like our child to receive Neurofeedback sessions (participation in project based on daily individual programming).**

Parent's signature: ______________________________

truth

hope.

love

407 HARDSCRABBLE RD. ROSWELL, GA · 770.998.1017 · www.JACOBSLADDERCENTER.com

Appendix B: Questionnaire instructions for parents and teachers (pre-assessment)

Dear Parents and Guardians,

Thank you very much for having your child participate in our research project.

In addition to the data we are collecting through our program at Jacob's Ladder, we also would like to track your child's progress based on an assessment provided by you as a parent.

Therefore we kindly ask you to fill out the attached questionnaires and **return** them to us **by Monday, June 17**.

Here are some hints concerning the questionnaires:

- ✓ Please make sure to **complete all items**. Only complete forms can be scored accurately.
- ✓ If you have any questions, please don't hesitate to ask us. To avoid missing items, we want to make sure that you feel confident with answering all questions.
- ✓ Please rate the items by **assessing** your child's behavior and skills **at the current time** (i.e. the last couple of weeks).
- ✓ Some items seem to be similar in their content. Please don't feel confused by that fact. Every single item needs to be completed and is important for the statistical analyses.
- ✓ If you have difficulties to rate certain items, do not contemplate for too long. Check the answering option that seems to be the most appropriate according to your personal opinion. Your first thought tends to be the most accurate.

If you are interested in any of your child's results, it would be our pleasure to discuss them with you after the completion of our research project.

Again, thank you very much for your participation!

Sincerely,

Karla Brigiotta Director of Clinical Services	Franziska Eller Intern/Teacher

407 HARDSCRABBLE RD. ROSWELL, GA · 770.998.1017 · www.JACOBSLADDERCENTER.com

Appendix C: Questionnaire instructions for parents and teachers (post-assessment)

truth **hope.** love

JACOB'S LADDER

Dear Parents and Guardians,

We are successfully conducting our research project your child is participating in and we recently recorded his or her second brain map.

As we mentioned at the beginning of the project, we would like to assess your child's progress based on an assessment provided by you as a parent.

Therefore we kindly ask you to fill out the attached questionnaires again to assess your child at the current time. Please return them to us **by Monday, September 23**.

Here are again some hints concerning the questionnaires:

- ✓ Please make sure to **complete all items**. Only complete forms can be scored accurately.
- ✓ If you have any questions, please don't hesitate to ask us. To avoid missing items, we want to make sure that you feel confident with answering all questions.
- ✓ Please rate the items by **assessing** your child's behavior and skills **at the current time**.
- ✓ Some items seem to be similar in their content. Please don't feel confused by that fact. Every single item needs to be completed and is important for the statistical analyses.
- ✓ If you have difficulties to rate certain items, do not contemplate for too long. Check the answering option that seems to be the most appropriate according to your personal opinion. Your first thought tends to be the most accurate.

If you are interested in any of your child's results, please let us know. It would be our pleasure to set up a short report about your child after the completion of the project and to discuss the results with you in case that further clarification is needed.

Again, thank you very much for your participation!

Sincerely,

Karla Brigiotta
Director of Clinical Services

Franziska Eller
Intern/Teacher

407 HARDSCRABBLE RD. ROSWELL, GA · 770.998.1017 · www.JACOBSLADDERCENTER.com

Appendix D: Modified version of the Autism Treatment Evaluation Checklist (ATEC)

Please indicate how much each statement applies to your child by checking one of the 5 boxes in every line below.

LANGUAGE & COMMUNICATION

	Not true		*Somewhat true*		*Very true*
Knows own name					
Responds to own name					
Responds to 'No' or 'Stop'					
Can follow some commands					
Can use 1 word at a time ***(No!, Eat, Water, …)***					
Can use 2 words at a time ***(Don't want, Go home, …)***					
Can use 3 words at a time ***(Want more milk, …)***					
Knows 10 or more words					
Can use sentences with 4 or more words					
Explains what he/she wants					
Uses appropriate gestures and facial expressions while communicating (verbal or non-verbal)					
Often uses several words or phrases repeatedly at a time					
Asks meaningful questions					
Speech tends to be meaningful/relevant					
Often uses several successive sentences					
Often only repeats phrases and questions of other people in conversations (instead of reacting, responding etc.)					
Carries on fairly good conversation					
Has normal ability to communicate for his/her age					

Are there any other special characteristics that you see in your child's language and communication despite the ones mentioned above? If yes, please describe:

____

____

SOCIABILITY & INTERACTION

	Not true		Somewhat true		Very true
Seems to be in a shell – you cannot reach him/her					
Ignores other people					
Pays little or no attention when addressed					
Uncooperative and resistant					
Does not show facial expressions or specific gestures in interactions					
No eye contact					
Prefers to be left alone					
Shows no affection, not touching or hugging					
Fails to greet parents and/or known peers					
Initiates contact with others					
Avoids contact with peers					
Avoids contact with family members					
Avoids contact with other adults					
Does not imitate (e.g. gestures, sounds...)					
Dislikes being held/cuddled					
Does not share with others (e.g. joy, interests, achievements...)					
Does not wave 'bye bye'					
Not compliant					
Lacks friends/companions					
Rarely smiles					
Does not respond to praise					
Insensitive to other's feelings					
Indifferent to being liked					
Indifferent if parent(s) leave					

Are there any other special characteristics that you see in your child's sociability and interaction despite the ones mentioned above? If yes, please describe:

____

____

BEHAVIOR & INTERESTS

	Not true		Somewhat true		Very true
Looks at people and animals					
Looks at pictures and books					
Looks at T.V. and computer screen					
Enjoys drawing, coloring, art					
Plays with toys appropriately					
Understands stories on T.V.					
Understands explanations					
Aware of environment					
Aware of danger					
Shows imagination (e.g. in make-believe plays)					
Initiates activities					
Dresses self					
Curious, interested, explores					
Venturesome					
"tuned in" – not spacey					
Struggles with fine motor skills, like handwriting					
Looks where others are looking					
Temper tantrums					
Seems to be very attracted by parts or details of objects (e.g. toys…)					
Needs a consistent and unchanging environment					
Needs a constant daily routine					
Has very limited interests (activities, toys, entertainment…)					
Often repeats specific body movements (e.g. flapping hands, tapping fingers, rocking…)					
Shows abnormal obsessive habits or rituals					

Are there any other special characteristics that you see in your child's behavior and interests despite the ones mentioned above? If yes, please describe:

____

____

HEALTH

Do the following **behaviors** and **physical conditions** describe challenges or problems in your child's life?

Please rate according to <u>these descriptions</u>: →

	Not a problem	Minor Problem	Moderate Problem	Serious Problem
Bed-wetting				
Wets pants/diapers				
Soils pants/diapers				
Diarrhea				
Constipation				
Sleep problems, can't get enough rest				
Eats too much/too little				
Extremely limited diet				
Hyperactive				
Lethargic				
Hits or injures self				
Hits or injures others				
Destructive				
Sound-sensitive				
Light-sensitive				
Bothered by textures on body, face or hands, having nails cut, hair combed				
Anxious/fearful				
Unhappy/crying				
Seizures				
Obsessive speech				
Shouts or screams				
Often agitated				
Not sensitive to pain				
Unaware of body sensations such as hunger, hot, cold, need to use toilet				
Cannot focus on interactions, tasks etc.				

Are there any other special characteristics that you see in your child's health despite the ones mentioned above? If yes, please describe:

____

____

Besides the enrollment at Jacob's Ladder, does your child currently get any other therapies or interventions?

If yes, please describe briefly what kind of therapy it is and the frequency of the sessions:

(Ex.: speech therapy, 2 times a week for 60 minutes)

____

____

____

____

Is your child currently on any medication that is related to his/her Autism Spectrum Disorder?

If yes, please name the drug and the purpose of its prescription:

____

____

____

____

Other comments (optional):

____

____

____

If you have any questions, please don't hesitate to ask.

Thank you very much for your time and effort!

Appendix E: Modified version of the Florida Apraxia Screening Test-Revised (FAST-R)

ID: ______________________

Date: ______________________

correct = completely correct response
related = accurate pantomime assoc. with target (but amplitude, timing, occurrence etc. incorrect)
nonrelated = real, accurate pantomime, but not assoc. with target
nonspecific = any reaction, but no real pantomime
no response = no reaction or unrecognizable response

***VERBAL COMMAND** (gesture to command, GTC)*

Show me how you...	*correct*	*related*	*non-related*	*non-specific*	***no response***
...wave bye-bye.					
...use a pencil to write on paper.					
...use a comb to fix your hair.					
...raise your arms.					
...blow a kiss.					
...use a key to unlock a door.					
...use scissors to cut paper.					
...knock on the table.					
...kick.					
...use a salt shaker to salt food on a table.					
...use a tissue to blow your nose.					
...cover your eyes.					
...stick your tongue out.					
...use a glass to drink water.					
...use a straw to drink out of a cup.					
...make a fist.					
...fold your arms.					
...use a knife to cut a pizza.					
...use a brush to paint a wall.					
...clap your hands.					
...use a spoon to eat soup.					
...use a toothbrush to brush your teeth.					
...stomp your feet.					
...tap your head.					

***IMITATION** (gesture to imitation, GTI)*

Do this...	*correct*	*related*	*non-related*	*non-specific*	***no response***
...wave bye-bye.					
...use a pencil to write on paper.					
...use a comb to fix your hair.					
...raise your arms.					
...blow a kiss.					
...use a key to unlock a door.					
...use scissors to cut paper.					
...knock on the table.					
...kick.					

...use a salt shaker to salt food on a table.					
...use a tissue to blow your nose.					
...cover your eyes.					
...stick your tongue out.					
...use a glass to drink water.					
...use a straw to drink out of a cup.					
...make a fist.					
...fold your arms.					
...use a knife to cut a pizza.					
...use a brush to paint a wall.					
...clap your hands.					
...use a spoon to eat soup.					
...use a toothbrush to brush your teeth.					
...stomp your feet.					
...tap your head.					

<u>DEMONSTRATION WITH TOOL</u> *<u>(gesture with tool use, GTU)</u>*

Show me how you use this.	*correct*	*related*	*non-related*	*non-specific*	***no response***
...use a **pencil** to write on paper.					
...use a **comb** to fix your hair.					
...use a **key** to unlock a door.					
...use **scissors** to cut paper.					
...use a **salt shaker** to salt food on a table.					
...use a **tissue** to blow your nose.					
...use a **glass** to drink water.					
...use a **straw** to drink out of a cup.					
...use a **knife** to cut a pizza.					
...use a **brush** to paint a wall.					
...use a **spoon** to eat soup.					
...use a **toothbrush** to brush your teeth.					

correct = completely correct response
related = accurate pantomime assoc. with target (but amplitude, timing, occurrence etc. incorrect)
nonrelated = real, accurate pantomime, but not assoc. with target
nonspecific = any reaction, but no real pantomime
no response = no reaction or unrecognizable response

Appendix F: Overview of the participants' relevant characteristics

ID	Group	Gender	Age (yrs;months)	Diagnosis	Co-morbidities	Verbal	Additional medication [1]	Additional treatments
01	treatment	male	10;11	Autistic Disorder	developmental language delay	yes	–	speech therapy (1x/week); occupational therapy (OT; 1x/week)
02	treatment	male	9;4	Autistic Disorder	–	yes	–	–
03	treatment	female	8;1	PDD-NOS	–	yes	–	–
04	treatment	female	8;1	PDD-NOS	–	yes	–	–
05	treatment	female	7;3	Autistic Disorder	ADHD	yes	Zoloft (50 mg); Intuniv (1 mg); Naltrexone (2 ml); GcMAF (8 ml)	speech therapy (2x/week); OT (1x/week); physical therapy (PT; 1x/week); ABA (2x/week)
06	treatment	male	4;7	Autistic Disorder	–	yes	–	speech therapy (1x/week)
07	treatment	male	6;8	Autistic Disorder	–	yes	–	–
08	control	male	7;2	Autistic Disorder	severe language delay	no	–	aquatic therapy (2x/week); speech therapy (1x/week); OT (2x/week)
09	treatment	male	9;2	Autistic Disorder	developmental coordination disorder	yes	–	–
10	control	male	7;10	Autistic Disorder	speech disorder	no	–	–
11	control	female	4;0	PDD-NOS	–	yes	–	music therapy (1x/week)
12	control	male	7;10	Autistic Disorder	significant developmental delay	yes	–	–
13	control	male	6;0	Autistic Disorder	–	yes	–	OT (1x/week); speech (1x/week)
14	control	male	12;4	Autistic Disorder	Staring spells	yes	–	–
15	control	male	14;4	Autistic Disorder	speech and language impairment	yes	–	OT (1x/week); speech therapy (1x/week); music therapy (1x/week); horse riding (1x/week); social skills training (1x/week)
16	control	male	7;6	Autistic Disorder	ADHD, speech disorder	no	–	–

Note: [1] Only those medicaments are listed that are prescribed for the diagnosed ASD or co-morbid mental disorders (not for other existing physical impairments)

Appendix G: Correlation matrix of gender, age and all subscales of the SRS-2, ATEC and FAST-R

	Gender	Age	SRS-2	SCI	RRB	I Lang [a]	II Int	III Beh	IV Heal	FAST-R	GTC_intr	GTC_trans	GTC_TOT	GTI_intr	GTI_trans	GTI_TOT	GTU_TOT
Gender	1																
Age	-.302	1															
SRS-2	-.342	.015	1														
SCI	-.294	.061	.994**	1													
RRB	-.496	-.176	.897**	.844**	1												
I Lang [a]	-.007	-.002	.639*	.659*	.485	1											
II Int	-.275	-.144	.737**	.738**	.640**	.561*	1										
III Beh	-.483	-.182	.683**	.643**	.762**	.668*	.717**	1									
IV Heal	-.185	-.234	.718**	.698**	.712**	.514	.720**	.719**	1								
FAST-R	-.149	.382	-.379	-.383	-.314	-.549	-.379	-.500*	-.341	1							
GTC_intr	-.070	.343	-.357	-.362	-.294	-.612*	-.351	-.458	-.325	.941**	1						
GTC_trans	-.356	.352	-.341	-.352	-.249	-.696**	-.247	-.404	-.380	.890**	.867**	1					
GTC_TOT	-.223	.360	-.361	-.370	-.280	-.681*	-.308	-.446	-.365	.947**	.965**	.967**	1				
GTI_intr	.044	.366	-.344	-.338	-.322	-.320	-.449	-.461	-.277	.901**	.853**	.633**	.767**	1			
GTI_trans	-.206	.427	-.368	-.374	-.294	-.359	-.411	-.461	-.324	.945**	.795**	.785**	.818**	.869**	1		
GTI_TOT	-.097	.413	-.369	-.370	-.317	-.352	-.443	-.477	-.313	.956**	.849**	.741**	.822**	.960**	.973**	1	
GTU_TOT	-.042	.230	-.328	-.327	-.290	-.465	-.269	-.540*	-.236	.922**	.808**	.784**	.824**	.795**	.889**	.875**	1

Note:
** $p < .01$.
* $p < .05$.
[a] $n = 13$

Appendix H: Results of one-sample Shapiro-Wilk test and Kolmogorov-Smirnov tests of normality as well as Levene's tests of equality of error variances

	Shapiro-Wilk test			Levene's test			
	Statistic	*df*	*p*	*F*	*df1*	*df2*	*p*
QEEG							
Delta - Absolute Power	.915	4	.511		-		
Alpha - Absolute Power	1.000	3	.972		-		
Alpha - Relative Power	.780	3	.067		-		
High Beta - Absolute Power	.970	3	.670		-		
High Beta - Relative Power	.889	3	.351		-		
	Kolmogorov-Smirnov test[a]						
	Statistic	*df*	*p*				
SRS-2							
SRS-2	.205	16	.071	3.091	1	14	.101
SCI	.179	16	.178	4.019	1	14	.065
RRB	.095	16	.200[b]	1.639	1	14	.221
ATEC							
I Lang. & Comm.	.141	16	.200[b]	5.802	1	14	.030*
II Sociab. & Interact.	.098	16	.200[b]	4.616	1	14	.050*
III Behav. & Interests	.125	16	.200[b]	8.947	1	14	.010**
IV Health	.155	16	.200[b]	4.974	1	14	.043*
FAST-R							
GTC_intrans	.147	16	.200[b]	.018	1	14	.897
GTC_trans	.351	16	.000**	.171	1	14	.686
GTC_total	.239	16	.015*	.011	1	14	.918
GTI_intrans	.257	16	.006**	.016	1	14	.902
GTI_trans	.182	16	.160	.023	1	14	.881
GTI_total	.216	16	.045*	.062	1	14	.808
GTU_total	.119	16	.200[b]	1.624	1	14	.223
FAST-R_total	.128	16	.200[b]	.028	1	14	.870

Appendix I: 2 × 1 repeated measures MANOVAs within the treatment group (n = 8): Results of univariate analyses for parent ratings and teacher ratings on the SRS-2 scales

	t1(pre) *M (SD)*	t2 (post) *M (SD)*	*F*	*p*	η_p^2
SRS-2 total score parents	110.75 (22.95)	95.50 (25.43)	5.157	.057	.424
SCI parents	87.75 (17.95)	77.13 (18.22)	4.595	.069	.396
RRB parents	23.00 (6.46)	18.38 (7.56)	4.912	.062	.412
SRS-2 total score teachers	110.13 (20.15)	83.25 (25.06)	8.180	.024*	.539
SCI teachers	90.38 (16.69)	68.75 (21.17)	6.587	.037*	.485
RRB teachers	19.75 (5.95)	14.50 (4.34)	5.948	.045*	.459

Note:
* $p \leq .05$.

Appendix J: Median values for all ATEC subscales for the parent and teacher ratings within the treatment group (n = 8) and results of the comparison of the two assessments at each time point (Wilcoxon Signed Rank test)

	t1(pre) *M (SD)*	t2 (post) *M (SD)*	*F*	*p*	η_p^2
SRS-2 total score parents	110.75 (22.95)	95.50 (25.43)	5.157	.057	.424
SCI parents	87.75 (17.95)	77.13 (18.22)	4.595	.069	.396
RRB parents	23.00 (6.46)	18.38 (7.56)	4.912	.062	.412
SRS-2 total score teachers	110.13 (20.15)	83.25 (25.06)	8.180	.024*	.539
SCI teachers	90.38 (16.69)	68.75 (21.17)	6.587	.037*	.485
RRB teachers	19.75 (5.95)	14.50 (4.34)	5.948	.045*	.459

Note:
* $p \leq .05$.

Appendix K: Median values for all FAST-R subtests and results of the comparison of pre- and post-assessments within each group (Wilcoxon Signed Rank test)

	Treatment group					Control group				
	t1(pre) *Md*	t2 (post) *Md*	*Z*	*p* *(2-tailed)*	*r*	t1 (pre) *Md*	t2 (post) *Md*	*Z*	*p* *(2-tailed)*	*r*
(a) Gesture to command										
intransitive	28.00	37.00	-1.96	.050*	-.69	12.5	27.50	-2.32	.021*	-.82
transitive	2.50	3.00	-1.76	.078	-.62	2.50	8.50	-2.21	.027*	-.78
total	29.50	37.00	-2.10	.035*	-.74	15.00	36.00	-2.52	.012*	-.89
(b) Gesture to imitation										
intransitive	41.00	45.50	-2.20	.028*	-.78	36.50	40.00	-.41	.684	-.14
transitive	29.00	32.50	-2.54	.011*	-.90	27.50	29.00	-.21	.833	-.07
total	69.00	78.00	-2.52	.012*	-.89	65.00	69.00	-.94	.345	-.33
(c) Gesture with tool use	30.00	37.50	-2.38	.018*	-.84	33.00	31.50	-1.05	.293	-.37
FAST-R total score	128.00	142.00	-2.52	.012*	-.89	111.50	131.00	-1.96	.050*	-.69

Note:
$* p \leq .05.$

Kolibri 360 GmbH
Ferdinand-Jühlke-Straße 7
99095 Erfurt, Deutschland
produktsicherheit@kolibri360.de